TAKE OFF YOUR
BLINDERS

Table Of Contents

Introduction

Chapter 1..............................Living A Clean and Holy Life

Chapter 2...........................Hearing The Voice Of GOD

Chapter 3..............................LETTING GOD LEAD YOU

Chapter 4.. Obeying GOD

Chapter 5...............................Change In Our Plans

Chapter 6............................Knowing Your Season

Chapter 7.........................The Pot "Satan's Playbook"

Chapter 8............................... SELF-FORGIVENESS

Chapter 9..............GET MOTIVATED AND GET TO WORK

Chapter 10...........................Being Used Effectively

Chapter 11..............................UNBLINDFOLDED

Dedication

I want to take the time to dedicate this book first and foremost to my Lord and Savior Jesus Christ for His continued wisdom, guidance and prayers. I also want to thank New Harvest Family Church (My HOME.) I want to give special thanks to my Mother and Father Bishop Dr. Carl and Lady Winona McCullen for raising me and teaching me how to be a man of God. I also want to thank all of my siblings, cousins, and friends (too many to name) who inspire me to raise the bar and fulfill my dreams. I want to give special thanks to my two sons C.J. and Kaleb for loving me. I am simply "daddy" to them and that makes me proud above all else. I want to thank Pastor G. Allen Jackson and the World Outreach Church for their support, wisdom, and prayers. Thank you pastor Allen for being an example and mentor. Also I want to thank Dr. George and Betty Jackson. Thank you everyone who spent your hard-earned money to purchase this book. Lastly I want to thank everyone who continues to cover me and my family in prayer on a consistent basis. Words cannot express my gratitude and humble appreciation. God bless you ALL.

I want to dedicate this book to the memory of my Cousin Gordon Christopher "Chris" Medlock. I miss you but we will meet again.

-C. Brandon McCullen-

Introduction

It is my sincere belief that the reason God inspired me to write this book is due to the fact that for the past 10 years or so I have watched and observed how the body of Christ has been blinded and manipulated by satan. He has somehow managed to deceive us and make us believe that we are doing what is right and following the plan of God when in fact we are not. Many Christians, unknowingly fall into this trap every day of their lives without even giving it a second thought. We go through our daily lives without even consulting God or asking HIM what He wants for our lives and what is our purpose in the earth besides the obvious mandate that Jesus commands that we be salt and light. Mathew 5:13,14.

What we really need to know about God's plan for our lives is right in front of us and all we need to do is seek him and ask for wisdom in His name Mathew 6:33 *but seek ye first the kingdom of God, and his righteousness; and all these things shall be added unto you.* God desires for us to seek after him for wisdom and look to him to guide us and trust that he is able to mold us into what he desires us to be so that he may get the glory out of our lives. It is our **RESPONSIBLILTY** as people of faith to accomplish our purpose in the earth.

God created Christians with PURPOSE in mind. No one's life is an "accident" we are all designed to fulfill our individual destinies and understand that the path that God has for us individually is very distinct and unique in its own way and not to be compared to the vision that God has for another person. It is my prayer that when you read this book, it will bring life to your spirit and enlighten your heart so that you may allow God to shape you into whatever he desires and that you will not be deceived and blinded by the spirit of decption.

Chapter 1

LIVING A CLEAN AND HOLY LIFE

In order to remove the blinders from our lives that are keeping us from fulfilling our God-ordained destinies, we must first learn to live a clean life that is holy and acceptable to God. God requires all of us as believers to live lives that are pleasing in his sight. Jesus instructs us that the first commandment is to love the Lord God with all of our heart, soul, and minds. He also tells us that if we love him we will keep his commandments.

How do we keep his commandments? By living a life that is acceptable to God. When we read the book of Romans chapter 12:1 we can understand that the apostle Paul explains to the roman church that they must present their bodies as a **living** sacrifice that is holy and acceptable unto God. When we study the word of God, we can see that in the bible days, people showed the Living God their love and appreciation by offering Him a sacrifice. These were usually animals such as bullocks, rams, and oxen in those days. They built altars and offered up these animals as a burnt offering to the Lord.

God still requires a sacrifice from you and I today, not with livestock, but rather with our own lives as believers. He wants our time, our worship, our prayer life, and our dedication and commitment to reading and studying his word. He wants us to make him a priority in our lives as believers. Many times the reason that we fall into sin and temptation is due to the fact that we do not make serving God our number one priority. God says in his word that He will not share His GLORY with another. Well how can we make God our top priority?

1. **The first step is realizing God's sovereignty and acknowledging His greatness and majesty**.

We must realize who God is and that before him there was no one else or nothing else. We must know that Jesus is the *author and finisher of our faith*. Hebrews 12:2. Notice that we always focus on the second part of that scripture text when we are quoting the bible but we forget the first part of that text that says *looking unto Jesus*. The only way to acknowledge that he is the author and finisher of our faith is by first acknowledging Jesus as the Son of God. *Jesus says that I am the way, the truth and the light. No man cometh unto the father but by me*. John 14:6. We must have a close and personal relationship with Jesus Christ in order to live a clean life. We must know who we are serving in order to live for him effectively.

2. Worshiping The Lord

The second way to live a clean and sanctified life is to worship the Lord daily. The bible says in John 4:24 that *God is a spirit: and they that worship him must worship him in spirit and in truth.* The first part of that reference is critical. It says worship him in SPIRIT. We must first learn how to tap into and access the heavenly realm where Jesus dwells in order to effectively worship him.

We must understand that worship is not always in the songs that we sing during worship services. We must understand that when Jesus worshiped God the father, he did not have musical instruments for his worship.

Worship begins in our hearts. God wants us to have a pure heart. The bible says in Psalms 24:4 *He that hath clean hands and a pure heart; who hath not lifted up his soul unto vanity, nor sworn deceitfully.* God wants our hearts pure and ready to worship him. Our worship comes from acknowledging that God is so much greater than we can even imagine him to be and that he must get the glory out of everything that we do.

In my own personal worship time, I always begin by saying; "Lord you are so wonderful to me." Father there is none greater than you." This gets God's attention. God loves it when we appreciate him just like we like it when someone esteems us and acknowledges us. Now I want you to understand that God does not at all NEED us, but he dwells in the midst of our praises. In other words God responds to worship. The second way to worship God is to thank him for all that he has done in your life.

In my opinion, it is a good idea to make a checklist of things that you are thankful for so that you can thank him for the things on that list and meditate on them. That scripture also tells us to worship Him "in truth." We must be sincere with our worship. Another way to worship effectively is to understand the meaning of the second part of that verse; "in TRUTH." This simply means to search the word of God and find the truth that is in the scriptures.

Many times we miss the blessings and favor of God on our lives because we do not take the time to read and study God's word. This is why the writer of the book of Hebrews chapter 11 verse number 6 wrote the passage; *he that cometh to God must believe that he is, and that he is a rewarder of them that diligently seek him.* Many times we do not read the word of God diligently. Sometimes we just simply read it. We do not ask God for knowledge and understanding. The bible says in Proverbs 4:7 *Wisdom is the principal thing; therefore get wisdom: and with all thy getting, get an understanding.* God wants to know that we are as concerned about getting to know him as we are about every other priority in our daily lives. The more we seek the presence of God, the more he will reveal to us. It is essential for us to understand and rightly divide the word of truth that is within God's word. This is what the apostle Paul meant when he wrote the second letter to Timothy, his Mentee in II Timothy chapter 5 verse 15. It is very important to show ourselves approved to God.

What that means is that as believers we have to prove ourselves to God. We have to show him that he can trust us with the things concerning his kingdom. It is extremely important for us not to lose sight of the fact that we must first be pleasers of Christ and later pleasers of man. That is why the psalmist David writes in the book of Psalm 118 verse 8 that *It is better to trust in the Lord than to put confidence in man.* God wants us to trust him first and everything else will fall into place. As I stated earlier, the bible says in Mathew 6:33 *"But seek ye first the Kingdom of God, and his righteousness; and all these things shall be added unto you"*. Well, how do you seek him first? By reading and studying God's word effectively and efficiently.

In the first step to removing our spiritual blinders, we must remember that it is important for you and I to live clean lives before Christ. Although we are not perfect, we must remember that God's word says that he is coming back for a church without spot or wrinkle. So we must take that into consideration as we live our lives from day to day. We must always consider Christ's way first and make it a priority to live for him unconditionally. This means that there are no stipulations to serving him.

We must live for him without expecting things in return. In other words we must live for him because we love him. God is not looking for the "perfect Christian" but what he is looking for is someone that puts forth the effort to be all that he or she can be for the kingdom of heaven. We must understand that we have an obligation to serve the most high. That obligation should not and must not be compromised. This is why God's word puts so much emphasis on living a holy and sanctified life. We must understand that we must follow Christ's example. Jesus was without sin. So, although we are not perfect, we should, without a doubt, be trying to live a life that is pleasing in the eyes of God no matter how trying and tempting the circumstances are.

Mathew's gospel gives a profound illustration of how Christ himself was tempted of satan in chapter 4. As we read the text, we will find that Jesus stood the course and his unwavering faith in his heavenly father was not compromised even though his body was in a weak state having fasted forty days and nights. That is why the devil came to him in that state. It is a fact that as followers of Christ we will be tempted on a daily basis. It is a constant challenge to live for God. There is nothing easy about living godly.

We will find many times as Christians that the enemy will always come to us when we are physically and emotionally week. In many cases, it seems as though whatever our flesh needs at the current time, the devil has it. What we must understand is that this is

NOT of God, it is in fact a blinder of decption. God wants us to deny our flesh so that we can hear from him. This is why Jesus tells us in Mathew 16:24 *If any man will come after me, let him deny himself, and take up his cross, and follow me.* If we want to follow Christ, We must deny or give up ourselves. We must relinquish our **fleshly** desires in order to be in right standing with God. God wants us to live pure and holy. So we must deny our flesh in order to line up with the plan of God for our lives.

Although the devil offered to feed Jesus and give him the land beneath the pinnacle of the temple, Christ's reply was that He would rather live by the word of God than live off natural food and self glorification. It is critical for us to see the world through God's eyes and that we aim to please him by avoiding and fleeing from the ways of the world. The bible says in Romans 8:6 *For to be carnally minded is* death; but to be spiritually minded is life and peace. There is no peace like the peace that you have in Christ Jesus. That is why the bible tells us in Philippians 4:7 *"And the peace of God which passeth all understanding, shall keep your hearts and minds through Christ Jesus.* In other words, we must rest in the fact that God will give us peace.

We must learn to let the peace of God guide us and lead us through our daily lives. We must trust in God's keeping power. That is why the bible says in Jude chapter 1:24 *"Now unto him that is able to keep you from falling, and to present you faultless before the presence of his glory with exceeding joy."* The devil's job is to get us carnally minded and wickedly thinking. If he can succeed in this area, he can get our focus off the things of God. Once he can manipulate and deceive us, he can destroy our vision and can block our divine purpose in the earth.

What we must do as believers, is not allow him to bring sin into our lives and blind our vision. Where sin is present, God is not. That is why God's word proclaims that if we do not have the spirit of God we are none of his. So we as believers must learn how to endure temptation and stand for what is right in the eyes of God. That is why the writer James wrote in the book of James chapter 1 verse 12 *Blessed is the man that endureth temptation: for when he is tried, he shall receive the crown of life, which the Lord hath promised to them that love him.* No matter what the temptation is, we must learn to overcome it. Living a blameless life before God is the key that unlocks the door to our destiny. Without living a clean and holy life, we cannot tap into God's promises. That is why the writer emphasizes *"to them that love him."* The bible says that if we love God we will keep his commandments. Loving God is obeying him. Obeying him is living a life that is holy before him. In Chapter 3 we will illustrate specifically how lustful sin and distractions can keep us blinded and stop us from seeing the will of God for our lives.

Chapter 2

Hearing the Voice Of God

The second way to remove our spiritual blinders is to learn how to effectively hear the voice of God. In this chapter we will discuss the different ways in which we can hear God's voice effectively. We will begin by illustrating how we get in position to hear God's voice. In understanding God's plan for our lives we must first be able to determine what the voice of God "really" is.

I will start by giving my own personal testimony. For many years of my life, I struggled with knowing the difference between hearing God's voice and hearing the deceptive voice of satan. Sometimes it was not even the devil. Many times it was just my own ambitions and dreams that I wanted to accomplish that were constantly in conflict with God's plan for my life.

Many times I would pray and pray and beg God to make these things come to pass. The problem with what I was doing was the fact that I did not even take the time to listen to what God was saying, I was so busy praying for what I wanted for my life without even hearing what God had to say about my life. For many years I had a prideful spirit that simply said; "This is MY life. I am an adult. I will do what I want to do with my life." The problem with that concept was the fact that I was not submitting to God's authority. I failed to realize that my life was Not MY life. Our lives are not our own. They belong to God. He controls our destiny. He has the blueprint for our lives before we are even conceived in our mother's womb.

The word of God tells us in Romans 8:14; *"for as many as are led by the spirit of God, they are the sons of God."* When I had my own life plan figured out, I was leaving God out of the equation. I was making it impossible for me to hear from God. My own personal agenda was always in the way of God's purpose for my life. One thing that I have discovered in the 25 years that I have been a Christ follower is that God does not impose his will on anyone. God gives us our own free will to make decisions with the lives we live. That is why the bible says in Joshua 24:15 *chose ye this day whom ye will serve.*

We must understand that as believers, we have an obligation to open our ears and hearts and be sensitive to what the Holy Spirit is leading us to do.

We must embrace the reality that God is always speaking. We must learn how to position ourselves to hear what he is saying to us.

1. Identifying God's Voice

The first way that we can Identify God's voice effectively is by reading God's word and understanding what God's role is according to what the bible says. The bible tells us that God's word will NOT return unto him void. As a result of this, we can understand that God's word is in fact TRUTH. It will stand the test of time. If you think that GOD said something and it turns out to be a lie, chances are it's NOT God's voice. If God says that something will come to pass then we can take it to the bank. It will happen PERIOD. God will not be mocked. God will not say one thing and then turn around and do another.

In identifying God's voice, we must be prepared to accept the fact that God may instruct us to do something that is contrary to our usual routine. When we study the word of God, we will find that in many instances God told his people to do things that were out of the ordinary in order to receive the blessings and miracles of God.

A perfect example of this is the miracle of the feeding of the five thousand. Jesus takes two fishes and five loaves of bread and feeds five thousand people. The bible even tells us that when they had eaten that there was still plenty of food left. Jesus took a little faith and met the need. All we need is faith and a need to hear from God.

Now, with that being said, we must realize that God may give us the answer that we need but not always in the manner in which we would like to hear.

God's ways are not our ways and sometimes what he wants for us and what we want for ourselves may not always be in agreement with one another. God knows us better than we know ourselves. He has specific plans and purposes for our lives that must be fulfilled. What we must learn is that sometimes God allows us to go through different situations that make us stronger in our purpose. Also the apostle Paul wrote in Romans 8:28: *And we know that all things work together for the good of them who love God and are called according to his purpose.*

What I have found is the fact that we read and quote that scripture all of the time as Christians but we don't take the time to fully understand what it means. There are three critical words in that scripture text. One of those words is **"ALL"**. When we meditate on what God meant when he inspired Paul to write that text that all things means all things. This doesn't mean that some things will work together and others will not. God wants us to trust his word. When God says something, he stands by what he says. This text clearly states that ALL things work together. So, when we understand that text we can fully understand God in his infinite wisdom. God will not leave us in a state of disaster. It is ultimately his will that we go through our tests and trials and come out victorious.

We must learn that as Christians we will have tests. This is why Peter wrote *Beloved thinketh it not strange concerning the fiery trials which is come to try you as though some strange thing happened to you. 1 Peter 4:12.* The harsh reality is that part of being a believer is going through tests and trials but we must consider that it is never God's intentions to keep us hanging in the balance. It is always His intent to bring us out of whatever we are facing. Our struggles are not meant to be permanent. John also wrote in John chapter 16 verse 33 *These things I have spoken unto you that in me ye might have peace. In this world ye shall have tribulation: but be of good cheer; for I have overcome the world.* We must know that in God we have the power to overcome. The bible also speaks of believers having the power to tread on scorpions and having the power to pick up deadly things that will not be able to harm us as Christ followers.

The second part of that scripture text in Romans 8:28 says for the good of them that **love God**. That part of the scripture cannot be ignored. If we don't love God, how can we hear from him and have faith in him? If we read Galatians chapter 5 verse number 22, we will find that love is the first fruit of the spirit. When you read the word of God, you will find that God usually puts things in order of importance. It is my firm belief that he put LOVE first because without love we cannot operate in any of the other eight fruits of the spirit. Without love we have no joy. Without love we have no peace. Without love we definitely don't have any patience, nor do we have gentleness, nor can we have goodness, faith, meekness or temperance. Having love for God and the things of God are extremely important. If we love God we will have no problem obeying the second commandment which is to love our neighbors as ourselves.

The third part of that scripture says: Called according to **HIS purpose**. This is why it is very important to understand what God is saying because many times we get lost in what OUR purpose is for OUR lives and we don't take the time to fully understand what GOD's purpose is for our lives. We don't take the time to get outside of our little box. We cannot step outside of this little picture of life that we have painted for ourselves. If we are totally honest with ourselves, this portrait of our lives doesn't really include God. It includes a form of godliness. In other words, a little bit of God and a whole lot of us. It's really more about what we want to accomplish for ourselves and has very little to do with what God wants to accomplish through us.

Now I am definitely not opposed to us having goals set for ourselves and going to school and getting an education as I did myself. What I am saying is the fact that every decision that we make as a believer, we should seek God first. What I have found is that we often times limit ourselves. If we would have followed God's plan for our lives, we would have been a lot better off than we would following our own personal agenda.

If we follow the apostle Paul's example in the book of II Corinthians 2:9 when he says; *But it is* written, *Eye hath not seen, nor ear heard, neither have entered into the heart of man, the things which God hath prepared for them that love him.* Many times we stand in the way of God's promises for our lives because we try to take control of every situation instead of allowing God to prosper us. We often times fail to realize that the increase and blessings come from the giver of the b*lessings and the increase.* Hearing from God is the key component in our quest for happiness. It is also necessary for our effectiveness in the kingdom.

2. What Do We Mean By Effectiveness in the Kingdom?

The reason is simple. If we are not following the plan that God has for our lives, we will not fulfill our purpose in the earth. What I have learned to know about God is the fact that he is very strategic in how he designs each and every one of us. When you read the scriptures, you will find that every anointed man and woman of God in the bible had a specific purpose and destiny. Moses did not have the same role as Abraham. David did not have the same role as Isaac and Jacob. Even though David and Solomon were both kings of Israel, they both had different purposes for the kingdom of God.

One of the best ways to understand this principle is by looking at the five-fold ministry. This is why the bible says that God gave *some apostles, some prophets, and some evangelists, and some pastors and teachers.* If God gave everyone the same gifting and talents a lot of needs would be unmet. It is God's ultimate plan for you and I to fulfill our purpose in the earth.

The body of Christ can be compared to the human body. The body needs a heart. The body needs a brain. The body needs lungs etc. If there are organs missing in the human body, it cannot function properly. The same principle holds true about the body of Christ. Everyone must do what they are designed by God to do. When Jesus left the earth in his ascension, he told the disciples exactly what he wanted them to do. He told them to teach all nations. This was a commission from God. When Jesus left the earth, the disciples knew EXACTLY what their purpose was. Now it is true that none of us have walked as closely with Christ as the disciples and seen him in the flesh as they did. What our goal should be is to identify the voice of God and to do as he commands us to do according to his word.

3. Follow What God's Word Commands us to Do

I have found that the best way that God speaks to me directly is through the scriptures. We must learn as believers that before we open our bibles and begin to read, we must ask God for revelation. God is constantly pouring out His spirit in the form of dreams and visions. What we must do as believers is learn to get in position to hear what God is saying to us. The best way that we can accomplish this is by allowing God to lead us through his word. That is why Christ made the proclamation that *man shall not live by bread alone but by every word that proceedeth out of the mouth of God. Matthew 4:4* What Christ is showing us through His bold declaration is the infinite wisdom that comes from the mouth of God, which is his word. His word is our daily bread. Christ rejected satan's offer to give Him natural food. He puts emphasis on the fact that it is more important to live by God's word than anything else.

I like to cross-reference the parable of the mustard seed according to Saint Mark's gospel with the story in the bible in which the disciples could not cast the spirit out of the young boy whose father came to Jesus. One of the reasons for which they could not cast out the spirit was the fact that they were operating in unbelief. Jesus tells them that if they would have faith the size of a tiny mustard seed that they could have the ability to move mountains. When you cross-reference that scripture, St. Mark speaks of the mustard seed as the smallest of all of the herbs but when it grows it becomes great and the fowls of the air can take shelter there. What he means is that the mustard seed faith MUST grow. It will not be as effective as God intended until it reaches its full potential. God never intends for our faith to stay as the size of a tiny mustard seed. He just wants us to start there. Our faith will grow with our knowledge of God's word. That is why the Apostle Paul wrote the passage; *So then faith cometh by hearing, and hearing by the word of God. Romans 10:17*

Hearing God's voice comes from having faith. Faith is obtained by our knowledge of God's word. This is why Jesus said *blessed are they which do hunger and thirst after righteousness: for they shall be filled. Matthew 5:6.* If we desire wisdom and knowledge it is available to us.

God loves it when we take the initiative to get to know him better. He rejoices over the fact that we seek to hear from him. When we look closely to the second part of that verse it says "for they shall be filled." This means that God will not hold back any knowledge from those who seek after it from him. God will continuously give us wisdom, guidance, and understanding if we just acknowledge his word and seek his presence. The more we desire the more we should study. The more we study, the more God GIVES!

Knowledge of God's word gives us wisdom and insight. It allows us to remain one step ahead of satan. When we are consistent readers and studiers of God's word we are not as vulnerable. We are not ignorant of satan's devices. It is as if we are more alert and on guard. The bible calls God's word the sword of the spirit. Without it we are going to battle unarmed and unprotected. This leaves us with nothing to fight the enemy with. We arm ourselves with God's word because the enemy is constantly attacking us. If we have nothing to decree or declare against satan, then we are not effective. This is why it is critical for us to get God's word on the inside of us so we can stand against satan. Nothing in, nothing out.

It is also important for us to study the parable of the farmer scattering seed. I will use St. Mark's account as an illustration. The farmer scatters the seed. The seed represents God's word. There are those in which the word fell on the ground but the birds ate it. These are those who hear the word but allow satan to take it from their hearts. Then there are those in which the seed falls on stony ground. These are those who hear the word and receive it with joy and gladness but they have no root. These are people who hear a great sermon but don't write any scriptures down. Whenever I am teaching a bible series, I always ask my students to take notes and write down what is being taught so that they can go back and study those scriptures that we discussed in class. This gives them a firm foundation to stand on so that they will not be so easily shaken and defeated. Then Jesus goes on explain those in whom the seed falls among thorns. These thorns represent challenges of everyday life and worries of the world that distract and discourage us from being productive in our lives. Although we hear the word, it is to no avail because our minds are so clouded with doubt, despair, and ambition. Then He tells of those who hear God's word and are fruitful because it falls on good ground. This represents the kind of Christ followers that we should always strive to be. When we receive God's word in our hearts we are fruitful and effective in whatever we do.

Another way that we can get in position to hear from God is by simply humbling ourselves. The bible says in 2 Chronicles 7:14 *If my people, which are called by my name, shall humble themselves and pray, and seek my face and turn from their wicked ways; then will I hear from heaven, and will forgive their sin and heal their land.* This scripture text in which God appeared unto Solomon by night, is still very important as it pertains to today's Christian. We still, at many times have a difficult time humbling ourselves. When you read this scripture text, you will find that God said "**humble themselves**, pray, and seek my face. The first part of what he is saying in my opinion is the most important.

When you really look at what he is saying here, the main way that God will respond and speak into our lives is by us simply getting out of His way. We must completely remove OURSELVES from the equation and submit to the spirit of meekness.

The apostle Paul puts it plainly in his letter to the Roman church in Romans Chapter 12 verse three when he says; *For I say through the grace given unto me to every man who is among you not to think of himself more highly than he ought to think, but to think soberly, according as God hath dealt to every man the measure of faith.*

God wants us to humble ourselves. God just simply will NOT agree with a prideful spirit. When we operate in this kind of spirit as a Christian, we make it virtually impossible to hear from God. God frowns on arrogance. Pride will block our destiny in a major way. God also emphasizes in II Chronicles 7:14 the need for prayer. Having a healthy prayer life puts us in a great position to hear the voice of the Lord.

When we pray, we open up a world of possibilities in the kingdom of heaven. We allow God to reveal things to us in the spiritual realm that we could not otherwise understand in the natural. In my own personal life, I have found that I have heard more from God when I am in constant prayer. Prayer is simply talking to God. This is why we must learn to ask God for wisdom and understanding during our prayers.

I have found that as Christians, we tend to focus more on what we don't have and what we want God to give us. Now this is important because the bible tells us to ask and it shall be given. We must look further than simply asking for what we need or want. We must learn to ask God to reveal his will for our lives. This is what I call "getting in position." When we "get in position", we allow God to show us his will for our lives. It is impossible to get in position without talking to God. When we are sincere and open up our hearts and souls to Him, God will reveal His will for our lives.

Our prayer is a major weapon against the enemy. Not only is it a weapon against the devil, but it also allows the Holy Spirit to warn us of dangers that are ahead. It allows us to see things before they happen and allows us to prepare for rough seasons in our lives. It also could just simply be a warning to avoid situations. There is nothing that I can imagine that is more important than hearing the voice of God. Hearing God's voice is essential. Nothing compares to it. Hearing God's voice allows so many possibilities in the kingdom of God.

The last part of that scripture says "turn from their wicked ways". As stated earlier, it is very important to understand that we cannot continue in sin and expect to hear from God. We must understand the root cause of where sin comes from. Sin comes from the devil. It is his primary goal to try to distract Christians from their purposes. If he keeps us in sin and wickedness, he knows that we won't hear from God effectively.

What I have discovered is that when we have sin in our lives it causes us to have what I like to call "mixed signals." In this state, the devil will have a field day with our psych. He can deceive us into believing what we are doing is "God's will" when in fact it is just the opposite of what God's will is. The way we give him the upper hand in our lives is by simply having wickedness in our lives.

This is why God told Solomon that if the people would turn from the wicked ways of the world that they would receive the blessings and favor of God. We must understand that God will not respond until we get rid of the blinder of unrighteousness that is blocking us from hearing God's voice.

In the chapters that follow, we will go into greater detail in describing specifically what some of the sins that cause our blinders to remain over our eyes are. We must comprehend the fact that hearing God's voice is essential and that he wants to talk to us. He wants to give us direction and wisdom. God just wants to do it on his terms and we have to allow him to do it by getting in position.

Chapter 3

LETTING GOD LEAD YOU

In the previous chapter we discussed ways to hear God's voice. In this chapter we will dive deeply into how we can effectively allow God to lead us as believers. We must understand that letting God lead us is an essential part of removing the spiritual and natural blinders from our eyes that make it virtually impossible to know what our purpose in the earth is.

Denying Flesh

In an earlier chapter, we discussed how we can get in the way of hearing what God is saying to us. We can also get in the way of letting God lead us as well. The first way we get in the way of letting God fully lead us into the way that he would have us to go is by submitting to the flesh. We must understand that God's principles nearly always depend on the sacrifices that we make as believers.

Earlier we discussed Romans 12:1 where the apostle Paul beacons the Roman church to present their bodies as a living sacrifice holy and acceptable unto God. We must learn how to bring our lives under submission to the Holy Spirit. This is why Jesus tells us to deny ourselves. This is an excellent example to follow as a believer. It is satan's job to keep us distracted by ourselves. He wants us to stay self-absorbed and self-reliant. If he can keep our eyes off of God, he will have the upper hand on us.

We must learn as believers to keep the spiritual blinders of flesh out of our vision. The bible tells us plainly that these distractions are: *the lust of the flesh, the lust of the eye, and the pride of life* I John 2:16. God's word tells us that these are NOT of God but rather of the world. The devil uses these things to keep us off course and away from our purpose and destiny. We will begin by defining each of these lusts and find the best solutions based on what the word of God says about each of them.

1. The Lust of The Flesh

The first of these lusts is the lust of the flesh. Mankind's struggle with the flesh dates as far back as the creation of Adam. When God made man, he created us from the dust of the ground. God made man in human flesh. All of the promises that we desired would be fulfilled and we could have whatever our heart desired without the penalty of sin. The problem came when Adam and Eve fell from grace. When this happened, it caused us to have the capacity to sin.

The human flesh became subject to the flesh. This justified the need for salvation. This is why Jesus paid the ultimate sacrifice for our sins at Calvary. When Jesus died, the veil form the temple was rent and it allowed us access to the kingdom of heaven. In the days of Moses, no one who was not of the tribe of Levi, the royal priesthood of the children of Israel, was allowed to go to God to make atonement for sins. It was, in fact, only the high priest of that tribe that was allowed to go into the Holy of Holies of the tabernacle. When Jesus Christ died for our sins he allowed us access to God our heavenly Father. The bible tells us in Romans chapter 8, verse 2 that *the law of the spirit of life in Christ Jesus hath made us free from the law of sin and death.* This simply means that the death of Jesus Christ validated our salvation. It broke the penalty of sin. When Adam and Eve sinned in the garden of Eden, they caused us all to be hell-bound and condemned. This made it difficult for us to live sin-free lives.

Now we must understand that as believers, although we do have the authority over the devil, we must not be ignorant of his devices (II Corinthians 2:11). The bible tells us that satan comes to kill, steal, and to destroy us. It is his responsibility to get us distracted from our purpose in the earth.

The way satan can keep us distracted is by getting us to yield to the desires of our flesh. I would like to take the time to share my own personal testimony concerning this matter. For a few years, I have been a single man. I struggled with the desire to be with a woman physically, emotionally, and spiritually for a long time. Instead of being productive and listening to God during my single season, I would always be focused on the fact that I was not married. For many years I would ask the questions; who, what, when, where? I later found out that what I was ultimately being driven by was the reality that I wanted to have a sexual relationship with a woman. Although I didn't act on those feelings, I sinned with my thoughts.

For a long time, I would allow the devil to continue to keep my attention away from God. I didn't realize that if a wife was what I desired all I had to do was ask in the name of Jesus and in HIS timing he would bring it to pass. So that is what I have done. I have decided that I am no longer going to allow the enemy to control my thoughts with lustful thinking. I have decided that when I feel that flesh is overriding God's calling on my life, I bring it under subjection and keep my focus on God.

That being said, some of us that read this book may not particularly have to deal with that aspect of fleshly lust. There are many other types of fleshly desires that keep us distracted. The first is what I like to call the **have not syndrome**. The have not syndrome focuses on what I DON'T HAVE in comparison to what others have. When I was growing up we used to refer to it as "keeping up with the Jones's." It doesn't matter how blessed we are, we always want what someone else has. Many times we will stop at nothing to get it.

T   his is due to the lack of realizing that we are blessed children of the most high God and that we are all unique in the way that God crafted us. We must understand that our purpose cannot be based on someone else's. We must find our purpose and stay on the pathway of righteousness. The bible describes this as coveting. We must understand that we cannot always have what someone else has. We must be content with what we have right now. Paul wrote in his writings to the church of Philippi that he had learned to be content in whatever state or condition he was currently in. In other words we must be always reaching and seeking to grow but we must accept where God has us during our current season without reservation.

When we follow the bible's example in II Samuel 11, we will see that the reason that David fell into sin is because he wanted another man's wife. That lustful, and fleshly desire over-clouded David's sound judgment. This caused him to take Uriah's wife and have him killed in battle. It is very easy to get entangled in a rat race to be the "most successful." In a fast paced society today, we are always trying to get ahead. Whether it is in corporate America or in our social status, we are always trying to finish first. It seems like everyone is trying to get ahead of each other today.

We must be thankful to God for what we have. We must learn to be content. I am a firm believer in self-improvement but must awaken to the fact that it should not be motivated by what SOMEONE ELSE has. The have not syndrome is the result of being driven by fleshly desires or "STUFF." This is why God wants us to seek him first. Prosperity given by God as a result of our faithfulness and commitment to his word is healthy. Prosperity driven by fleshly desires is NOT of God. This also qualifies as being lust of the flesh.

Many times we are naturally inclined to think of sexuality when we think of lust of the flesh first without understanding that there are other components to this fleshly desire as well. With the example we used earlier about King David lusting after Uriah's wife, we can plainly see that David, not only lusted after another man's wife, he also coveted his wife. He wanted what someone else had instead of looking to the giver of the blessings. We often times make the mistake again and again of trying to have exactly what someone else has instead of looking to Jesus as our **source**. He gives us what HE desires for us to have if we are faithful to believe Him for the manifestation of it.

Another example of the lust of the flesh is **negative thinking**. It is the devil's job to get us thinking negatively. If he can get our attention off of what God can and will do, he can blind us from our purpose. This is why the bible tells us in Hebrews chapter 11 verse 35 *Cast not away therefore your confidence, which hath great recompense of reward.* God wants us to understand that our confidence in his word pays great dividends. There is a great reward associated with having faith in God.

We must hold fast to the reality that our faith in God's promises is what powers our success in the kingdom of God. If we have NO faith, we have NO strength. Negative thinking and negative speaking are wholly associated with the flesh. When we read further down into the next chapter we can see that in verse 6 of the eleventh chapter it reads *"But without faith it is impossible to please him:* Simply put, we must put away all negative thinking and focus on what God can do. We will find that the more we keep our focus on the things of God and the more we put our trust in him, the easier it is to live.

I have found in my own personal walk with Christ, that when negative thoughts try to come to me, I immediately take authority over them. I immediately rebuke the source of the negativity, which is **SATAN,** by the blood of Jesus Christ. Once I have taken authority over my thoughts, I immediately start to fill my mind with positive thoughts. Once I have done that I begin to fill my spirit with scriptures that support positivity. We must learn that the number one way that the devil uses to attack us spiritually is through our thought process. If he can control our thoughts, he will succeed in knocking us off course on the road to our purpose.

2. The Lust of the Eye

Another type of lust that the enemy uses to keep us from letting God use us is the lust of the eye. We as believers must learn that the eye can be deceptive. It can deceive us by making us believe that what we are seeing is something inspired by God when, in fact, it is the opposite. For example: Someone goes into the local supermarket and only has $5 of spending money. There are two choices that he or she can make. One of them is an unhealthy food item that is packaged very well and the other is a healthy food item that is not quite as presentable in its packaging. The temptation is the unhealthy food item that will kill us in the long run. The only problem is that we cannot see it being harmful long-term. We can just see how attractive it looks right now. As a result we make the WRONG choice, when the right one was right in front of us all along.

This is how the enemy is successful in taking us off course in route to our purpose. He can make the wrong choices look like the right ones and with our EYES it looks so much like the wrong choice is the correct choice. This is why we, as believers, must pray for spiritual discernment. We must be able to hear God's voice when it looks so much like the wrong choice is the right one. Satan is so good at his job of deceiving that it will make the wrong choice look like it is the will of God. He will even make provisions that appear as though we are experiencing the "favor of God", when God is not at all involved in the situation.

This is why the bible tells us in Ephesians 5:15 *See then that ye walk circumspectly, not as fools, but as wise.* The following verse tells us that the day is evil. God wants us to use wisdom in the choices that we make. The bible also tells us to watch and pray. This means that sometimes we may, in fact, have a great prayer life but we are not watchful.

Christians that are not watchful are open prey for satan's attacks. This is exactly what the enemy wants. He wants us to take our attention off God. This is why Peter began to sink. When Jesus stretched forth his hand and commanded Peter to come out into the sea to walk on water, Peter was okay as long as he kept his eyes on Jesus. The moment that his attention left Jesus, he began to sink. He lost his focus because of things that were going on around him. So many Christ Followers today are still like Peter. We allow the enemy to take control of our eyes. This causes confusion. The bible tells us that God is not the author confusion. This means that where there is confusion, God cannot be present.

In this portion of the chapter we will discuss the two types of lust of the eyes. The first lust of the eye is the:

Natural Eye

We as believers must understand that the devil will use things to tempt us that we can see with our natural sight. I first want to start by dispelling the myth that: " **Once we are saved, we are no longer**

tempted by the things that we did before we became born again." This is why the bible tells us in the book of James 1:12 *Blessed is the man that endureth temptation: for when he is tried he shall receive the crown of life, which the Lord hat promised to them that love him.* God is not at all impressed with those of us that are "Holier than thow." He wants to see who can endure the temptation and stay on the path of righteousness.

It is a fact that the devil will not use things that we are not attracted to as a method of deception. He will in fact use those things that we love the most and that are most attractive to our eyes. The fact of the matter is that the devil knows what we like. He knows what appeals to our flesh. The enemy knows just how to package things to make them look attractive to us.

The devil will continue to throw things in front of us that are appealing to us that can steer us away from our purpose. We must always be on guard. When we see something that appears too good to be true, we must always ask the question: "What does God's word say about this?" We must always look to Jesus for our answers. We must have a CONSISTANT prayer life. We must also flood our spirit with the word of God. This is why Jesus declared that man MUST live by the word of God as well as natural food.

Distractions that the enemy uses in association with our natural ability to see can cause us to fall into temptation every time. We must be able to identify what is of God and what is not of God. Once we are able to distinguish when God is moving in our lives and motivating us to do something and when the enemy is trying to deceive us into believing that what we see is in fact of God, we can live as much more effective Christians. We will not be so easily deceived into believing satan's lies all of the time.

The second type of lust of the eyes is:

Spiritual Eye

In the previous illustration, we partially dealt with this aspect. Although natural eyesight and spiritual eyesight have similarities, they are also very distinctive in nature. The spiritual eye in fact deals primarily with the things that we see in the spirit. In Galations 5:22, the Apostle Paul explains to us that the fruits of the spirit are: *love, joy, peace, longsuffering, gentleness, goodness, faith, meekness, and temperance.* All of these fruits don't necessarily apply to the natural senses but do, however, apply to the senses and emotions associated with the spirit. Spiritual eyesight ties in with the fruits of the spirit.

The way we view things spiritually affects each and every fruit of the spirit.

We must learn to see ourselves as Christ sees us. If we don't see ourselves as He sees us, we cannot walk in any of the fruits of the spirit. The enemy can very easily control our spiritual eyesight as well as our natural sight. I will use my own personal testimony as an example: When I was younger in my faith, I used to think that people had negative thoughts about everything that I did. Many times that did not hold true. Most of the time it was my own personal insecurity that allowed me to think that someone was always out to get me.

The enemy deceives us by making things APPEAR to be things that they are not in the spirit as well as the natural. The problem with what I was seeing in my thoughts and spirit was the fact that I didn't see myself the way that God saw me. The bible tells us that Jesus sees us as more than conquerors. It also says that God sees us as the "Royal Priesthood." In Romans 8:17, the apostle Paul wrote that God sees us as joint heirs with Jesus Christ. This is an awesome phenomenon. The idea that God sees us as an heir to his inheritance with his beloved son Jesus Christ is AMAZING. We must see ourselves as an heir. Once we know who we are and who's we are, we can conquer anything.

I have found that If we see ourselves as GREAT in the eyes of God, we can obtain a higher level of faith. This is why Jesus tells his disciples that if they would have faith the size of a mustard seed that they would have the ability to move a mountain. Mountains can only move if we see ourselves as Christ sees us. This is what will help us grow and blossom into the spiritual conquerors that God's word declares that we are.

We must understand that it is important for our spiritual eyesight to be intact. We cannot allow the enemy to deceive us into believing that we are less than what God's word says we are. We must see ourselves as the heirs to the kingdom that God sees us as. Once we can see through the eyes of God, we can take control over the false perception of reality that satan throws in front of us on a daily basis.

The final blinder we will deal with in this chapter is:

THE PRIDE OF LIFE

One of the biggest things that cause Christians to fall short in their walk with Christ is the principal of PRIDE. The enemy uses pride constantly to attack believers and to distract us from our purpose in the earth. We must learn to bring pride under control if we want to let God lead us into our destiny. The bible teaches us that PRIDE comes before destruction. This is an unfortunate reality because there are so many people on the road to destruction today as a result of prideful living.

In overcoming pride, we must first understand the principle of humility. The Apostle Paul includes humility (meekness) as one of the fruits of the spirit in Galatians chapter 5. In analyzing this principle it is important to realize that if God places humility in the scriptures in such an intentional way, he wants us to apply it to our lives.

When we study how King David was chosen in the bible to reign over Israel, we can see that Samuel found him in the field tending to his father's sheep.

David was simply being mindful of the responsibilities that his father had given him. He was acting in the spirit of humility and obedience, this caused God to smile upon him and to be pleased with his actions. As a result God chose him to be the next King after Saul.

God is not looking for the prideful Christian. He is simply looking for those who will work in the kingdom and humbly submit to his authority. If we want the blessings and favor of God on our lives, we must understand that there is a price. That price is the price of humility. If we take down of ourselves and submit completely to the Holy Spirit, he can fully use us in the capacity that he has chosen us for. This is why the writer Paul wrote in the book of Ephesians chapter 4 verse 1; *I therefore, the prisoner of the Lord beseech you that ye walk worthy of the vocation wherewith you are called.* The apostle Paul is telling the church of Ephesus that it is important to be worthy of their calling.

Well how are we worthy of our calling:

1. Through humbling ourselves
2. Studying the word of God
3. Finding our purpose
4. Living a life that is pleasing to God.

We have already discussed the importance of humility. Now we will briefly discuss objectives 2-4.

Studying the Word of God

This is a critical component to walking worthy of our calling. The only way that we can walk worthy of our calling is by knowing what our calling is. The way that we find out what our calling is comes by finding out what God's word says about us. God's word lays the foundation of Holy living. With no holy living, we cannot effectively walk worthy of our callings.

Finding Our Purpose

We cannot fully understand the principle of walking worthy of our calling without knowing our calling. This is why the bible tells us in 2 Peter 1:10; *Wherefore the rather, brethren, give diligence to make your calling and election sure: for if ye do these things ye shall never fall.*

This scripture can be taken to mean two things: One is obviously talking about making sure that your life is in order. The other God gave me through revelation means simply being sure about what our calling and purpose in the earth is. That is why it concludes by saying that if ye do these things ye shall never fall. This simply means that if we are operating out of sync with what our calling is, we throw everything out of order. This causes us to fall because we are not acting according to what God has commissioned and ordained us to do. This is why we must always be sensitive to what the Holy Spirit is saying at ALL times. It is imperative that we know what our calling is.

Living a Life that is Pleasing to God

We must always know that above all other priorities that our number one priority is to live a clean and sanctified life before God. If we do not follow this principle, we ruin our influence and our saltiness. I will briefly share my own personal testimony concerning this matter. Several years ago, there was a fellow musician that I used to collaborate with and knew very well amongst the circle of musicians in the industry that we all knew. This gentleman was a "struggling" Christian. He believed in

God and was saved but he was a backslider. He struggled with drug addiction among many other things. He, often times looked to me for spiritual guidance and prayer.

During this season in my life, I was around 21 years old and was still toying with the ways of the world. I really wanted to serve the Lord with all of my heart, but I still had some issues that I was dealing with. There were some things that I didn't want to let go of. Sometimes I would find myself sneaking out to the clubs and parties with my "Christian friends." Just when I was in the middle of my partying and having a "good time" I saw this very same gentleman that I was witnessing to. Although he didn't say it, I know that he was disappointed with me. I was the one person that he felt he could go to for spiritual advice and here I was in the club getting my GROOVE on. The feeling that I had that day was the worst feeling I had in my entire life. I felt like I had failed him. I felt I had failed myself, and most importantly that I had failed GOD. It was at that moment that I made up in my mind I was going to be a for real Christian. I would no longer compromise my influence.

This is what Jesus Christ did. He lived a life before his peers. He set an example for the disciples and every one that he came in contact with. This is why he was so anointed. He was tempted but did not yield to that temptation. He would not compromise his relationship with his heavenly father. This is the example that we must follow as Christians. Falling into sin is NOT worth the cost of losing our influence.

As we stated earlier, our influence is very important and we must let our lights shine and never let them go out. We must understand that as children of God, we are always going to be under a "microscope". Everything that we do is under surveillance. This is why Mathew's gospel chapter 5 verse 14 declares; *Ye are the light of the world. A city that is set on a hill cannot be hid.* In other words, he likens our influence to a city that is set on a hill. This means that no matter what we do, people are constantly watching our lifestyles. They are constantly watching our behavior and how we govern ourselves as children of God.

We MUST understand that as children of God, we are the most influential people in the world. This is why God charges us with such a great responsibility to live a blameless life before those who do not know him. We must realize that our focus on what GOD wants for us is more important than any other priority in life. We must realize that he expects excellence in how we live our lives and how we influence those around us who do not know Jesus as their personal savior.

Often times when we read this passage in the book of St. Mathew, we read verse 14 but we don't read down to verse 15 which reads; *Neither do men light a candle, put it under a bushel, but on a candlestick; and it giveth light unto all that are in the house.* We must not hide our salvation, but instead we must make it available to anyone who needs it. We must proudly live our lives as Christians, those who are called and chosen by God. If there was ever a time when we should live holy before God, it's right now. With everything that is going on in the world it is indeed our responsibility to lead those to Christ who do not know him.

We must understand that every point discussed in this chapter is essential in letting the Lord lead us to our destinies. We must understand that God should always be the driver in our vehicles of life. Never once should we put our hands on the steering wheel and try to take over what God should be in control of the entire time. In taking off our spiritual and natural blinders it is key that we grasp this concept moving forward. In the next chapter, we will deal with the principle of obedience and what steps we should take to being someone who walks in obedience.

Chapter 4

OBEYING GOD

In taking off our blinders that block us from our destinies, we must understand that it is extremely important for us to become children of obedience. In 1 Peter 1:14, the bible tells us that we must consider ourselves as obedient children. The bible tells us that obedience is better than sacrifice. When we see the prophet Isaiah call the children of Israel a sinful nation in the first chapter of Isaiah, he goes down through the text and explains how God would rather have us obey than to offer up a sacrifice. Now with that being said, we must first analyze what sacrifice meant to God.

When we read the word of God, particularly in the old testament, we will find that when sins where committed and when the children of Israel wanted to receive something from God, often times he required a sacrifice. The best cattle were usually required as a burnt sacrifice as we discussed earlier. You will even find that the prophet Elijah in the book of I King chapter 18 offered up a sacrifice to the Lord to prove that his God was superior to the 850 prophets of Baal's. These people worshiped a false god named Baal. God used the prophet to show the people how important sacrifice is to him. As a result of this sacrifice, he showed them that he was the only supreme GOD. Once the sacrifice was offered, THEN and only then was God's presence manifested.

If God wants his people to give their best for a sacrifice, it is clear to see how he values sacrifice. Now if the bible tells us that obedience is BETTER than sacrifice, we can draw the conclusion that obedience is a very serious principle of being a follower of Christ.

When we look at what happened to Moses in the bible when he did not do as God had instructed him to do, it cost him a trip to the land of Canaan. This was the land that God had promised the children of Israel. What's alarming about this is the fact that Moses was a man whom God had chosen to lead his people out of Egypt. Moses did not speak to the rock out of anger and decided to strike it twice. That was a blatant act of disobedience and thus cost him access into the Land God promised him. Also when we look at the account in I Samuel chapter 15, we see how Saul tried to cover his disobedience by offering sacrifices with what God told him to destroy. Samuel then tells him that God says that it is better to obey than to sacrifice. Saul did not destroy ALL of the Amalekites as God had instructed him but he instead spared the king and the finest oxen. He then tried to offer those oxen as a sacrifice even though God told him to destroy EVERYTHING including the king and his children and ALL of the animals good and bad.

God has not changed his feelings about obedience. We MUST understand as Christians that if we want to fulfill all that God has called us to do for his kingdom, we must learn to walk in obedience. Disobedience is the biggest **blinder** in Christian's lives today. It is one of the number one reasons that we miss our destinies. Sometimes obedience might be something as simple as telling someone about Christ today or even washing a sink full of dirty dishes. We must realize that God values stewardship. We cannot be so consumed with our spiritual lives that we forget the natural ones. God will hold us just accountable for things such as not paying our bills on time, and not keeping our houses and cars clean. This constitutes disorder. God doesn't like disorder. When we are out of order, we are also operating in disobedience and this will cause us to miss our blessings. In my own personal journey I, for so many years, found it difficult to follow order. I could preach, play instruments, and prophesy, but my house was a mess and my bills were always late. I always wondered why I could never seem to get ahead until the Holy Spirit revealed to me that God was NOT happy with the way I was handling business. God's word tells us that God rewards those who diligently seek Him.

When we study the word of God, we will find out that the simplest disobedience caused great men of God lots of misery. When God tells us to do something, we must know that is exactly what He expects us to do. So many times we find ourselves trying to blur the scriptures and bend them to fit our own personal agendas. We don't even take the time to properly interpret the scriptures and ask God for TRUE revelation. This is why the bible tells us to *"Rightly divide the word of truth."*

What steps do we follow to be someone who walks in obedience?

1. Accepting God's Word as TRUTH

In removing the blinders from our lives we must know God's word is in fact TRUTH. We must understand that every word that is written in God's word is true. This is why the bible tells us in John 8:32 *And ye shall know the truth, and the truth shall make you free.* When we read this, we can come to the conclusion that God is showing us that knowing and understanding TRUTH will allow us as believers to be FREE.

I also want to touch on an earlier verse in the same passage of scripture when Jesus tells the people in verse 24; *I said therefore unto you, that ye shall die in your sins: for if ye believe not that I am he, he shall die in your sins.* God is showing us the importance of believing in his son Jesus Christ. Jesus tells them that if they don't believe that he is the Messiah, they will die in their sins. Believing is critical because, according to God's word, if we don't believe, we will miss out on the kingdom of heaven.

The bible also tells us in Proverbs chapter 1 verse 7 that *the fear of the lord is the beginning knowledge; but fools despise wisdom and instruction.* In other words, if we respect the things of God and listen to his council and take his word as TRUTH we will have understanding and knowledge but if we don't obey, we will be considered to be as fools. This ties back in to John 8:24, if we don't believe we will die in our sins. How will we die in our sins? We will die as FOOLS.

In order to obey God's commandments, we must know what God's word says and accept it as truth. If we don't know what God commands us, we cannot walk in obedience. The key is: KNOWING. After we know, then we must DO. That is why God's word tells us to be hearers and doers of the word. This is why the enemy makes everything in the world come up in our lives when we are trying to sit down and study God's word. He doesn't want us to KNOW. If he can keep us from KNOWING then he can keep us from DOING what God commands us to do as Christians. This is why we must overcome our flesh and have a set time that we devote to prayer and studying God's word. This time MUST NOT be tampered with, nor compromised. This must be a sacred time that we get in the presence of the almighty God to obtain wisdom and knowledge from him. Nothing should be a priority over our time of devotion.

God's time must not be compromised. The time we spend with him is sacred. This is where we can receive the insight and direction from him. Getting in God's presence can, in many ways, overpower the negative voices that are contrary to God's will. These voices can confuse us and keep us off the course of fulfilling what God wants us to fulfill. When we study God's word, we eliminate confusion from our lives. We must remember God is NOT the author of confusion. If there is confusion about a decision or an idea that we have about a "ministry" idea, we must reevaluate our decision. This means that we need to go back to the "drawing board" and seek God's face a little while longer. Knowing that God is not the author of confusion is vital to accepting God's word as TRUTH. The second way that we can effectively obey God is by:

2. Trusting God

I have found that it is extremely difficult and in many cases impossible to obey someone that I do not trust. A major part of following someone's leadership is learning how to trust them. With that being said, in order to TRUST God, we must know what his track record is. We find this out by knowing what his word says about what he has done. This is why as we discussed earlier, Romans 10:17 faith cometh by hearing and hearing by the word of God. Well let's take a moment to evaluate what God's word says about his track record. If God can take a poor little

Hebrew boy named David and transform him into a King over Israel, and can take a man named Moses who had an identity crisis to lead a multitude of Israelites out of Egyptian captivity and then have his successor named Joshua lead them into the promise land, and can take a young woman by the name of Esther that wasn't even on the King's radar to be his wife and transform her into a queen, then we can realize that whatever we need Him to do, He has the capability to perform it. This is why God's word declares; " Being confident of this very thing, He that hath begun a good work in me shall perform it until the day of Jesus Christ." Phillipians 1:6.

We must understand that God is not at all concerned about what our background or genealogy is. He does not care who we come from, nor is he concerned with whether or not our parents sinned or what they were. When God CALLS us, he has a specific purpose in mind. God is faithful to carry out that purpose in our lives. He just wants us to allow him to. Allowing God to use us means that we TRUST him. We must learn that God's way is the ONLY road map that leads to eternal life. Without HIS guidance we cannot make it to heaven.

I have learned that when I am NOT totally yielding to the Holy Spirit and not allowing God to be first in my life that I have NO peace. The bible tells us in Phillipians 4:7 "And the peace of God, which passeth all understanding, shall keep your heart and minds through Christ Jesus." In other words, the peace that we have in God far transcends any other peace that we can imagine. This peace is so AMAZING. It keeps us in the will of God. It keeps us hearing from God and obeying His commandments. It causes us to be in a place where we come to the realization that everything that we have accomplished and that we have succeeded in is all because of Him.

3. Avoiding Sin

In my opinion, sin is the number one thing that keeps believers from walking in obedience. Many times, the reason that we cannot act on what God has instructed and commanded us to do is because we have sin in our lives that needs to be removed. This sin becomes a stumbling block and a distraction that keeps us away from fulfilling our purpose.

We must not allow ourselves to fall into the pitfalls of sin because it can set us off course and cause us to lose a lot of valuable time. Sometimes the penalty of sin is far too costly. Many people die before they reach their purpose often times because they are deceived and feel as though they are unworthy of forgiveness therefore they continue to live sinful lives that often lead to a tragic end. Many people die in sin without fulfilling their destiny because they don't realize the fact that God is full of grace and mercy.

Often times the only thing that God wants us to do is just simply repent. This is all he asks of us. God's word tells us that if we repent that He will do the rest. (1 John 1:9). If we would simply repent, then God will forgive us. As a matter of fact He has already forgiven us but we don't even realize it. We spend so many years of our lives wallowing in depression and self-pity. This causes us to lose so many years of our lives that we could be using for the glory of God.

The awesome thing about God and His love, grace and mercy is that once we have repented and been forgiven, we are right back where we are supposed to be. Once we are in ORDER, then God can put us right back on the path of our destiny and purpose.

The key part of understanding our purpose is being in God's PERFECT will versus the PERMISSIVE will. The perfect will of God gets us an all-access pass to our blessings and favor. This constitutes COMPLETE obedience. When we are completely submissive and obedient to God then that opens up an enormous realm of possibilities. When we read and study God's word thoroughly, we find that God's complete favor ALWAYS followed obedience. When we line up with the perfect will of God we allow Him to work in us and through us at full capacity. This is when the windows of heaven are opened up completely and blessings are poured out. As Christians we love to quote Malachi 3:10 where it talks about the windows being opened but we fail to read the earlier part of the verse where the conditions apply. What God has shown me over the years is the fact that although salvation is free, prosperity and favor cost. There is always a cost involved. That cost is obedience and order. For an example, I have two sons, one is 11 and the other is 12. In our house we put a great emphasis on education and the importance of academic excellence. Sometimes they perform better than others, but they both realize that when they receive good grades, they are rewarded. Although it does not cost them a dime to live at home, it does cost them to receive the benefits of performing well in the classroom. God is the same way with us, there are some of us who are definitely born again but are not walking in the PERFECT will of God. These people are walking in the permissive will only. Although they may in fact be blessed, they will NEVER fully obtain all that God has for their life until the completely submit.

I had an encounter with a man at the gym that I work out at one day. We were sitting in the Sauna. After a hard workout I was extremely tired. At the time, I was at a very difficult season in my life. I wasn't sure what God was saying and I was feeling frustrated, depressed and discouraged. The man that was in the sauna with me spoke a word into my life that I will never forget. He told me "young man, God has great things in store for you beyond your wildest imagination". He then took me to Jeremiah 29:11. He then told me that God will only do these things in my life when I totally submit to Him. When he first said that to me, I was slightly confused because I thought that I was doing everything that I possibly could do to please God.

Shortly after that encounter, I began to pray and ask God to show me the things that I was doing that were hindering my blessings and favor. God began to show me little by little the things that I was doing that seemed small to me but were not so small to Him. These "little" sins and acts of disobedience that seemed so minor and irrelevant to me were hindering my blessings. God was not pleased with me because my life was out of order. I was still traveling the nation preaching and teaching the gospel and recording music that glorified the name of Jesus but there were still some things in my life that needed to be corrected. As a result God was NOT going to allow me to prosper with those things out of order.

The bible tells us in Romans 6:23 that the wage (penalty) of sin is death. This doesn't always, however mean a natural death but it can equate that. The bible tells us that our bodies are dead because of sin. The deception that is prevalent with today's ministry is that we are not teaching the principle of living godly lives as Christ followers like we used to. It seems to me as though we put so much emphasis on prosperity but we leave out the fact that God's word clearly tells us that we MUST walk uprightly in order to receive the full blessings and benefits of being a Christ follower.

Sewing and reaping does not always mean giving of monetary possessions but also giving our lives completely over to God. When Paul wrote in Romans 12:1 about presenting ourselves as **LIVING** sacrifices unto God, he was clearly dealing with giving of our lives and not our possessions. God's word tells us that God is a rewarder of those who seek Him diligently. So God truly values those of us who live Godly and pure before Him.

Often times as believers, we get discouraged when we see those who are walking in sin appearing to prosper when we seem to be living stagnant lives. It is extremely important for us to keep our priorities in perspective. When David wrote Psalm chapter 73, he described seeing the prosperity of the wicked, he even admits that he almost slipped in envy and jealousy because of the evil that they were doing and still prospering. The lesson in what was written in this passage is that he said that he **ALMOST** slipped. It is ok for us to hate sin if we are followers of Christ. If we follow Christ we should hate sin. It is our duty. In the hating of sin, we must not, however, allow ourselves to get envious against the wicked. In Psalm 37 and verse one it is written that we must not be jealous or envious of those who do evil because they will soon be cut down as the grass and wither away. The bible also tells us that the pleasures of sin are only for a season. This means that it is only temporary and must come to an end at some point. Then Jesus tells us that the meek shall inherit the earth. We must maintain a spirit of humility, love, and godliness, even toward those who we know are living sinful lives without remorse.

The important thing for us to understand is that seasons do not last forever but rather are only for an allocated period of time such as: Summer, Spring, Winter, and Fall. They soon come to an end. Sometimes God gives us "grace periods" to allow us to get our houses in order. The prophet Isaiah came to Hezekiah and told him that he had to get his house in order because he would soon die. That was a period of grace allocated to him because God wanted him to be in right standing before his time was up. Even though God granted him an additional 15 years, there was still a specific timeline that he had to follow in order to get things right. Many of us, however, are not as lucky as Hezekiah. We don't know how long our "grace period" is but we must understand that we are living on borrowed time when we are out of the will of God and our sins will, in time, catch up with us.

No one is exempted from the penalty of sin. It is a reality that we must all face if we don't get our lives in order. We must realize the seriousness of this reality and not take our lives for granted. In closing remember that every minute and every second that you spend walking in sin and disobedience is time wasted.

Chapter 5

Change in Our Plans

When we are young children in grade school, we often times dream of how we want our lives to go. We have our entire future planned out and sometimes our plans are well organized and thought out. We often times plan our lives as follows; When we graduate from high school, we will go to a certain University of our choosing and obtain a bachelors degree in pre-med. From there we decide that we are going to attend medical school at Harvard for example. Then we will do our residency for 2 or 3 years and from there we will move to a city where we will practice medicine. From there we will meet the man or woman of our dreams and get married. Then we will have 2 or 3 children and live in a big house on the hill with a 4 car garage and lots of money and savings and live happily ever after and then GOD's plan for us enters the equation and everything changes.

While our plans may be good plans that are well organized and dreamed, they may not necessarily be God's plans for us. Someone once told me that the best way to make God laugh is to tell Him your plans. At the time I didn't really get it but since I have seen God completely redirect my course in life for His glory I can see the truth in that statement. I am not against dreaming. There is nothing wrong with dreaming, in fact the bible tells us that without a vision we will perish and then in Habakkuk 2:2 it tells us to write down our vision. Even though this is true and

God does honor our diligence and preparation, we must be open- minded about what God wants out of our lives as believers.

When we really look at the entire picture, our lives are not our own, we are chosen and appointed by God for a divine purpose. The paths that we choose are critical in understanding what God has for us. We remove the **blinders** from our eyes when we are in sync with God's plan for our lives. When we are certain about what He wants us to do, we save ourselves years of heartache, frustration, and disappointment.

Success and fulfillment are not always measured by how much money we earn. For example: I know doctors and lawyers who wish they had not chosen the carrier path that they chose. The fact is they were NOT CHOSEN by God to pursue these professions.

They simply chose these paths because of the earning potential and social status that they would obtain. Whenever we are not walking in our divine purpose and calling, we never feel fulfilled. Something always feels empty.

I have found that in my own personal life, God does not let me prosper when I am not totally yielding to His will. He blocks my success and does not allow me to succeed at whatever it is that I am trying to do that is contrary to what he wants out of my life. It does not matter whether it is a business venture, a ministry idea, or a degree I wish to obtain, when I am not walking in the complete will of God I will NOT prosper. I used to get angry and frustrated when this would happen but now I have learned to be grateful when this happens. Many times God has a way of protecting us from our own selves. Sometimes God can be like a mother that slaps her child on the hand to prevent them from touching a hot stovetop. He knows that it will be harmful for us to choose a path that He did not ordain so He prevents us from succeeding because He loves us.

It is extremely important that as Christ followers, we get a clear understanding of what GOD wants to accomplish through our lives. We must seek him diligently and pray for clear understanding. We must seek wisdom and guidance from the Holy Spirit about everything that we do. He must be our life tour guide. Without His direction we are lost and blindfolded.

When we read in God's word in Philippians 4:6, the passage begins by telling us not to be anxious for anything   but to seek God through prayer and petition. Many times we make hasty decisions in our lives without being open-minded about what God wants from us. We make impulsive decisions that can sometimes take us years to recover from. For instance, you may have enough money and good enough credit to finance a $300,000 home with a 15 year mortgage at 2.5 percent. You decide as a family to pray about that purchase and God says wait and don't do it. You may decide to go ahead and do it anyway instead of accepting the wisdom of the Holy Spirit. At the time that you make the purchase you have a household income of around $185,000 per year. Mathematically that makes sense but what happens when one or both of you loses a job? Now you can only get a job paying half that amount. Now you have a big mess to clean up that can cause not only financial problems but emotional strain on your family. God sees what we can't see. He knows what is awaiting us down the road. We must first realize that our lives are not our own and that God has chosen us with a specific purpose in mind to fulfill HIS glory in us. Often times we lose focus on this when we are planning "our" futures. Many times God is nowhere to be found in our life plans. Before we chose a career, start a business, or have a ministry vision, we must first take it to the Father. God's word tells us in Romans 8:30 *Moreover whom he did predestinate, them he also called: and whom he justified, them he also glorified.* In other words, God already knew us and predestined our lives for HIS glory. What we must learn to do is get in line with the glory.

Getting in Line With God's Plan

In order to figure out what it is exactly that God wants out of our lives, we must learn how to get in line with His plan. The best way is to start by being very candid with God. Just simply ask Him what He desires for your life and how He wants to fulfill it through you. In doing so, be prepared for God's honest response. We must be opened to the fact that when we truly hear from God about what HE wants out of our lives that He may tell us to get rid of some things that we might not want to get rid of. Remember the story that I told earlier about the encounter with the man at the gym when he told me that I had to submit to God's will. This really applies when we get to the stage when we are truly ready to hear from God. Usually God will begin to reveal to us things that we must purge or take on to get in line with His will.

Purging

Let's begin with purging. Merriam-Webster's dictionary defines the word purge as to "purify". This is a great place to start in removing blinders from your eyes. This is especially a good place to be if you are a brand new Christian. The bible tells us that when we are in Christ we are a new creation and that the old things are gone and ALL things become new. In order to maintain a healthy relationship with Christ, we must make everything around us NEW. This can include old friends that do not mean us any good and or acquaintances and places that always remind us of what we once were. These things carry spirits that are familiar to what identified us as sinners. Now that we are Christ followers, He is now our identity and everything that we are associated with MUST reflect Him.

In the previous chapter we discussed obedience and how sin can distract us from hearing clearly from God. One of satan's number one strategies is to make us believe that it is completely harmless to still be around our same friends and acquaintances and stay a healthy and productive Christ follower at the same time. We lie to ourselves when we say things such as; "I will go to the bar but I won't order a drink, I will give him or her my number but we won't hook up, I will still hang out with my old gang but I won't do what they do." This is a HUGE deception and a lie perpetrated by satan. The longer we associate ourselves with what we used to be, the more likely we are to fall back into our former wickedness. The bible tells us in the 1st chapter of the book of Psalms not to walk in the counsel of the ungodly nor to stand in the way of sinners. It is very critical to realize that we are influenced negatively and positively by those who we surround ourselves with.

Whether you are new Christians or you have been in your faith walk for a while, it is always a good practice to surround yourself with positive people and places. When you are trying to get clarity and understanding about what God wants to do in you and through you it is important to surround yourself with like-minded, Christ-centered people. Healthy relationships with like-minded Christians are important to have. They will help mold, encourage, and inspire you to grow and cultivate and mature the gift or gifts that God has given you.

In doing so you must also be aware that sometimes like-minded is not always healthy because if you are a needy person with low self-esteem it's not always a good idea to connect with people who are EXACTLY like you. It's usually a good practice to be around people who are where you **desire** to be.

I will give my own personal testimony as a point. When I was trying to change seasons in my life, I had to disconnect from people who were, in fact, Christians but they were not necessarily at a point in life that I was trying to go. While they were good people, they still had characteristics that reminded me of my old mindsets and philosophies as well as some of the bad habits and addictions that I was trying to overcome. When God is trying to move you to a new season in life, sometimes you have to make a faith move. Sometimes you have to move to a different city, change your surroundings, find a new job, get some new friends that have what you want. My parents always instilled in me the importance of dreaming big. They also told me that if I wanted to be successful, I had to be around people who were successful. It is important to have at least one person in your life who is a model of what you want to accomplish according to what **GOD's WILL** is for **YOUR** life. It's always a good habit to find out what makes them tick. Find out what their success model is, what their failures were and how they overcame them. The more you learn, the less likely you are to repeat some of those mistakes.

Get Knowledge and information

Always remember that knowledge is power. Once I began to hear from God about what He wanted from my life, I began to search for knowledge. I would find books and articles that were related to what I wanted to accomplish. I began asking necessary questions and gathering as much information associated with my purpose and calling.

It is also important not to waste time doing nothing when you should be gathering resources and getting the necessary education that is required for you're life mission. Often times getting knowledge may include going back to school and obtaining a degree that will give you the credentials that you need to achieve what you have been predestined to do. I always tell children when I travel this nation to always pray and ask God for guidance concerning what degrees that He wants you to pursue and obtain in college. It would be pointless to get a degree in education if God has called you to be a psychologist. Quite often we waste so many years of our lives going down a path to nowhere because we do not consult God about what He wants out of our lives. The bible tells us in James 1:5 that if any man requires wisdom to ask of God who will give it freely and not withhold it. God just wants us to ask Him what He wants out of our lives. Often times we as believers like to quote Proverbs 3:6 but we don't really acknowledge Him nor do we really let Him direct our paths.

Don't Try To Be What Your FAMILY Wants You To Be

Quite often, if you are not careful, you can allow the pressure of what your parents or other family members have accomplished to dictate what you are in life. You are unique in nature. God created YOU for a specific purpose that He wants for you to accomplish. If your mother is a doctor and your father is a civil engineer that does not mean that is necessarily what God has predestined you to be. It is important to hear from God. He is your guide. You must fulfill your purpose. You were created for a different purpose than your parents.

Even if you do end up being a doctor like your mother, you will NEVER be the same type of doctor she is. Even if you go into the same field of medicine, there is always going to be a different method to what you do. Find out what your divine purpose is and pursue it with all of your might. Do not allow the pressure of "legacy" and "tradition" to **blind** you from what God is trying to show you. You cannot afford to waste years of your life trying to satisfy what someone else feels is your purpose in life.

Don't Give God Credit For What He Did Not Orchestrate

A common mistake that I have seen so many Christians make is giving God credit for something that He did NOT ordain. We often times have an infallible tendency of saying that God lead us to do something that He clearly did not. The interesting thing that I've observed is that when the results don't turn out as we think they should, the first person who gets all of the blame is God. We give Him credit and then we blame Him when He is responsible for neither.

Most decisions that are impulsive are usually not God-Driven. These are usually decisions that we think are best for our lives and we usually have not consulted God regarding them. Quite often we don't pray long enough and we don't give God a chance to respond. I sometimes believe that many times we just pray to ease our conscience. We are simply going through the emotions and not really meditating or seeking God for answers concerning His will for our lives.

Not knowing what God is saying clearly can cause a great level of frustration for many of us. This is why we must be consistent with our fasting as well as praying and studying God's word. The fast literally crucifies the fleshly man. Jesus told His disciples that they must deny themselves in order to follow Him. A fast causes the denial to take place. When the denial takes place then the flesh becomes submissive to the spirit. When the flesh submits to the spirit, then it becomes much easier to hear what God is saying through the Holy Spirit. When we are in tuned with the Holy Spirit we are able to communicate with God. The Holy Spirit is like a translator between God and man. He de-codes what God is saying and makes it clearer for us to understand what is being spoken.

"Every good idea is not a God Idea"

-Angus Buchan-

In this chapter we have been discussing how sometimes we as individuals will have an idea of how we can have our lives planned full of wonderful ideas and innovations. Sometimes, although we have great ideas and creativity, these ideas are not God-ordained. Just because it's a good idea doesn't mean it's a God idea. There are so many dreams and aspirations that we have as individuals. As people we are naturally inclined to dream. It is AWESOME to be a dreamer. God gives us the ability to dream.

What we must consider as people in search of finding God's plan for us is the fact that our ideas should ALWAYS line up with what our calling is. Sometimes we allow ourselves to get entangled in things that are ungodly and our focus comes off of the things of God. Before we put any idea into effect we must ask God if He approves of what we are trying to do. We must get in tuned with the Holy Spirit and allow Him to lead us. The bible tells us in Philippians 2:5 *Let this mind be in you which is also in Christ Jesus.* Once we take on the mindset of Christ then we can get in tuned with what God is saying and our ideas will begin to line up with His will. God's word also tells us in Romans 8 that God conformed us into the image of His son. In other words God wants us to think like Christ. He wants us to have God-driven, God-focused thoughts and ideas. Ideas and dreams that line up with what **God** purposed us to do please Him.

We allow ourselves to take on the mind of Christ by spending time in his presence. For instance, the more time you spent with your spouse, the more you learned about them. The more time you spend with your children, the more you understand their behavior patterns and how they think. The same thing holds true with God. The more we are in His presence and are meditating, praying, reading and fasting, the more we will have a clear understanding of what He wants out of our lives. This will help us take on the mind of Christ because we will know the plans and purposes that He has for our lives without being blinded by satan.

What Ideas are God Ideas?

God ideas are ideas that come directly from the inspiration of the Holy Spirit. Typically these ideas will bring our spirits to a peaceful state. When we are doing things that are not God-Driven we will typically have an uneasy feeling. It usually feels like we have butterflies in our stomach and we are unsettled. Something feels wrong but you can't quite put your finger on it. Although satan is a masterful deceiver he is not at all smarter than God. He always slips up and shows his hand. When an idea drops in your spirit and you feel total peace and joy with no reservations chances are that is a GOD idea.

You must be extremely careful though because sometimes God ideas will make you nervous as well. This is usually because sometimes they will require a major leap of faith and will challenge your comfort level. Usually when this happens to me there is a reassurance from God that He is working on my behalf and everything is working together for my good. In other words, do not give in to fear and intimidation.

How to Avoid Ideas That Are Not God Ideas

As I stated earlier ideas that line up with the will of God please Him. It is extremely important for us as Christ followers not to waste valuable time being entangled with things that are not focused towards fulfilling our divine destiny. It can be extremely difficult sometimes to hear from God concerning what He wants out of our lives. Usually everyday responsibilities can be a distraction. Even though we MUST go to work every day, pay our bills, raise our children etc., we must always have time to focus on building a strong and healthy relationship with God our father. Sometimes going on a fast and meditating gets our focus back to where it needs to be.

I have found that in my own personal life when I hit a roadblock or a difficult decision in my life it usually means that it is time for me to fast. When I fast it gives me a renewed and refreshed feeling. It helps me get back to where I need to be to receive and hear from God.

The enemy can flood our minds with all types of things that have absolutely nothing to do with where God is leading us. These things cause a major distraction and the time we spend trying to "resolve" them we miss what God is trying to do in our lives. Let us briefly discuss things that we must avoid and the things that we must do in order to keep our hearts and minds open to receive what God is doing in our lives.

1. Don't Let Personal Struggles Cause You To Lose Your Authority

For so many years of my life the devil could always keep me from hearing from God by attacking me personally. It would usually be a sick relative, financial stress, something regarding my children's mother, or my children having struggles in school. Honestly when things are not going right in our lives, it can be extremely difficult at times to hear from God.

It would always seem as though after I would preach an awesome sermon or write an amazing song and God would use me in a miraculous way to show his glory, the devil would come after me full throttle. Even though I knew the attack was coming, I was not properly prepared to deal with it because I didn't understand the power and authority that I had as a follower of Christ. As soon as the struggles

124

would come, I would quickly try to find, on my own, a way to "put out the fire" quickly so that I could move back in to what God was leading me to do. When my solution to the problem didn't come immediately, I would become extremely frustrated and disheartened. This would either cause me to become enraged and vengeful, or discouraged and depressed. When I would yield to those spirits I would give over to the flesh. When this would happen then I was out of position to hear from God because I lost my AUTHORITY.

It almost felt as though I was in a continuous cycle. This would happen over and over again. I would get really focused and intense about my purpose and all of a sudden challenges would come and I would lose my authority. It seemed as though I would NEVER get out of that cycle.

One day God took me to Matthew 6:33 *But seek ye first the kingdom of God and his righteousness; and all these things shall be added unto you.* I had grown up in the church, so I had heard that scripture thousands, if not millions of times. One day God completely opened my eyes with full revelation of that bible verse. He showed me that if I would keep my focus on the things that pertain to God and what He had chosen me to do, then He would take care of the minor details that seemed so large to me. When I received that word, I began to view my life differently. Although most of the problems still existed, I no longer saw them as a major concern anymore. I would just simply take them to God in prayer and allow Him to give me direction concerning how to resolve the issues. Meanwhile I got MORE passionate about my purpose and began to exert all of my attention on what God wanted from my life. My problems no longer defined who I was.

The devil wants to keep us bound as Christ followers. If he can keep us depressed and discouraged then he can keep us distracted. This is an age-old tactic that he has used since the days in the Garden. The devil wants to take away your confidence. Remember the verse we discussed in a previous chapter from the book of Hebrews chapter 10 that tells us not to cast away our confidence. The confidence is not in our own ability but rather in Christ's ability to use us in the way that He chooses. When we allow God to lead us and remain in control of our lives, there is nothing that is too great or impossible.

2. **Don't get distracted trying to support someone else's vision!!!!!**

I have found personally that one of my biggest weaknesses is my passion for seeing people pursue their purpose. I love to see someone doing something for the kingdom of God. I enjoy supporting people's ministries and seeing them accomplish their goals in life. I am a **life coach** by nature. I love helping others.

Sometimes being passionate about helping other people can take our attention away from what God has called us to be. It can keep us off of our own path. I used to spend so much time day and night supporting other people's visions. I would help them organize events, play the piano for them, speak at their events and write songs for them while my own ministry and vision would sit on the back burner. Other people's visions and ministries would always take priority over my own.

I was missing my own season focusing on helping everyone else's visions when God was pulling at my heart and telling me that it was time to be preparing to be used in my own calling. Before I move any further, I do want to set the record straight. I am not saying that we shouldn't be a help to someone occasionally, but it shouldn't take priority over what we are RESPONSIBLE for doing for ourselves.

In fact God has actually assigned some of us to some people to help their ministries. Some of you are a Silos that is assigned to a Paul. Some of you will spend your lifetime playing a role in another person's ministry. That is completely acceptable if GOD has ordained that, but you should ask God for the wisdom and discernment to know the difference.

Our time is way too valuable to allow others to get the best of what GOD wants to use. When we deplete all of our energy and resources helping other people's visions and ministries, we are too exhausted to use them for what God wants.

Chapter 6

KNOWING YOUR SEASON

In removing the blinders from our eyes that keep us distracted from what God has purposed us to do it is critical for us to know **WHEN** it is time for us to move in our season. The major inspiration for the writing of this book was someone very close to me who moved out of season and started to pastor a ministry before his time. He left the local ministry where he served and took his entire family out of the church to start his own work. I do believe in my heart that God may have very well called him to be a pastor but the timing was not right. In this chapter we will discuss how we will know when the timing is right and what God's word says concerning it.

Reason and Responsibility vs. Passion

I want to begin this chapter by addressing the issue of reason and responsibility vs. our own passion. It is amazing to be passionate about what God has called you to do. There is absolutely nothing wrong with being passionate about our calling in life. In fact God gets the glory when we are passionate about our purpose. One thing that we must be aware of is the fact that the devil also knows that we are passionate and anxious about what God has called us to do. He will try to cause us to move ahead of our season to accomplish our mission.

Although we may in fact be called to do what it is that we are moving ahead of God to achieve but the season is just not right yet. Remember how we discussed in a previous chapter the haves and have-not? What often times happens is that the enemy will show us what everyone around us is doing. He will lie to us by telling us that we should be doing what they are doing right NOW. It is usually something that we are called to do that they are doing. We see them prospering in their ways and we begin to try to emulate them and do what they are doing. All that we can see is that they are doing what WE are "SUPPOSED" to be doing. Usually we are correct in our assessment but it's not time for us to move. God is still preparing us for the path that HE wants us to take. We spend so much time trying to keep up with what everyone else is doing that we lose focus on what God is trying to work out in our OWN lives. This anxiety and ambition drives us to move when God has not given us permission to.

Sometimes we see where they are but we don't know what they had to do to get it. We don't know how they had to prepare for the blessing that God has given them. We don't know the things they had to overcome or the struggles that they faced on the road to their success. On the flip side what glitters is not always gold. They may not be doing as well as they may appear to be doing. They may not be as successful as you think they are. They might have a great big church in a nice neighborhood but they have a great big financial mess to clean up. They may have a congregation full of people but it might be a congregation full of hell raisers. Before we evaluate and assess what everyone else is doing, we must take a personal inventory of our own lives.

Many times the reason why God is not using us as quickly and aggressively as we would like is because He is simply preparing us. We are still in the preparation and development stage of our lives. We are still in elementary school spiritually and we want to graduate from Harvard with a Ph.D. tomorrow. Just because God is saying NO right now to our wants and desires, it does not necessarily mean that it is a long-term no. God is protecting us from destruction because He knows that if He gives us a responsibility that we are not ready for, we will ultimately mishandle it.

God tells us in His word that his thoughts for us are of peace and not of evil. Let us examine that briefly. When we look up the word peace in the dictionary it is defined as a state of tranquility or quiet, freedom from civil disturbance. Merriam Webster's describes it as having a state of tranquility and quiet with NO disturbance. When we are letting God prepare us and are moving in HIS timing as opposed to our own we are in a peaceful state of mind. It is much easier to follow the will of God than to go contrary to it. God gives us all free will. He will not impose His will on any of us but when we chose to do things our own way and not follow God's formula for our success, we enter into a world of problems and disturbance. We open up a Pandora's Box of dysfunction and misfortune in our lives. When we completely flow in the direction and timing that God has for us we are at a much more peaceful level.

As believers many times we want a microwave ministry. We want the success but we don't want the suffering that births the success. God's word tells us in Psalms 34:19 *Many are the afflictions of the righteous: But the LORD delivereth him out of them all!* We want the success but we don't want to go through the tribulations and trials that lead to the success. So when we have a clear understanding of what God has for us, it is much easier to accept the concept of timing. God has thoughts of peace and happiness for us, not of evil. God is not trying to "block our happiness" but rather protect us from things that he knows that we are not mature enough to handle at the present time.

God does in fact want to see us happy. He wants to see us fulfill our divine purpose and calling. God just simply wants to see us achieve it when we are in a season that will maximize our potential. When we wait for the right time to let God use us then we are allowing him to use the very BEST of us and not a microwave version of us. We should ask ourselves a simple question: Does God really want to use a

person in his kingdom who is not mature enough nor prepared for the job. It's almost like a person starting a new job and the first day on the job they are elevated to upper management without the proper skills or training. This is a bad reflection on the company. It shows lack of leadership. If they are letting people get promoted that don't deserve to be then it will cause a major break down in the flow of the corporation. Nothing will flow right if a piece of the puzzle is out of place. The same thing is true about our gifts and callings. There is no way that God will promote us to a higher level of ministry when we are not good stewards over what we currently have. God will NOT take us higher until we have completely matured and are ready for the task at hand.

MARRIAGE

I wanted to dedicate a portion of this chapter to this topic because it holds a special place in my heart. This is an area that I, like so many Christ followers, have been deceived in. One of the biggest areas of deceptions that satan has and is still using to deceive Christians is knowing the RIGHT season to get married. If you are single and seeking marriage this section is for you.

When I was around 21 or 22 years of age I began feeling a strong desire to be married. I began to look at Proverbs 18:22 *"Whoso findeth a wife findeth a good thing and obtaineth favor of the LORD."* Even though my desire was godly, the timing was not. I began to see my friends getting married around me and I began to long for marriage so desperately that I would almost stop at nothing to accomplish it. I wanted to be just like everyone else. I wanted the happiness that I thought they had. I wanted someone to hold, hug, kiss and to love. I also wanted to be loved by someone. I wanted someone to spend the rest of my life with but I was not prepared and the **TIMING** was **NOT** right. As fate would have it, I did in fact meet the woman that I believed at the time that God had placed in my life. We were married after only a little over a year of dating. There were **MANY** red flags and warning signs that this was not a person that I should be yoked with but I simply ignored them and married her anyway because I did not want to be lonely. Four years later I was a broken divorced single father trying to raise an infant and a toddler by myself. I am extremely proud of my two sons. I know that they are a gift from God and I love them with all of my heart but I now know that I could have made better life choices. Being a single father now is a **DIRECT** result of my disobedience and inability to wait for God to bring His promise to pass.

Let us examine what God's word says about what we should be doing while we are single and believing God for our spouses. In Colossians 3:2

God's word tells us to keep our affections on the things of God and not the things that pertain to the world. When our minds are on the things of God and not on wishing that we were married then it is extremely difficult for the spirit of loneliness to overtake us. When that spirit becomes dominant in our lives it causes us to make hasty and irrational decisions. We make choices based on our emotions and not on what God wants to accomplish in our lives.

Many times when we are dealing with the topic of marriage, we ask ourselves over and over again the questions: why is God making me wait so long? Why won't He give me what my heart desires? Let's take a look at Psalms 37:4 *Delight thyself also in the Lord and He shall give you the desires of thine heart.* That scripture is cut and dry. When we keep our focus on God and take delight and joy in what we do for Him, He will freely and joyfully give us what we desire. If your desire is to be married, keep God first. Let him fill the void of that mate that you desire.

When we are on the road to our destiny and operating in our divine timing and purpose, there is nothing that God will withhold from us that He promised. Almost everyone that I know who has a healthy, godly marriage says that they were not seeking a mate but rather seeking God when they found them. When we are seeking God and what He desires for us it is almost as though the very thing that we believe Him for creeps up on us when we are not even searching for it. We are not even aware of it. When we stop focusing on who, what, when, where and why or how and allow God to move in His timing we will have so much peace and tranquility. God knows what we desire and He wants the best for us. He just simply wants the best for us at the RIGHT time. God's timing is the BEST timing.

Don't Try To Speed Up The Molding and Learning Season

Another common mistake that we make when we are anxious about being "used of God" is the fact that we do not allow God to work things out in our lives. There is a lot of growth and development that has to take place during our preparation period. There are so many issues that God needs to deal with in us before He can release us to do whatever it is that He has called us to do.

When we look back at the earlier point, God will not move us until we are ready. Many times there are issues that affect us that we have no control over. These could be things such as: family history (the way we are raised), child abandonment issues or even various types of abuse that we might have encountered. Sometimes we have issues in our lives because we are victims of someone else's negligence. These issues can often take many years to work through. God cannot release us to do certain things if He knows that we are still dealing with these issues. Sometimes we may still be harboring unforgiveness towards the person or persons that may have wronged us. This can hinder our progress because God does not want you and I being damaged goods trying to preach, teach, or lead His people with all of those unhealed scars.

In other cases we can also be dealing with issues that WE caused ourselves. I have found that when I am at fault and my blessings are being hindered because of me, I make a habit of immediately trying to repent so that I can stay in right standing with God. When we are out of order God will not bless us. God's word says that He will not withhold any good thing from those who walk **uprightly** before Him.

This means that there are criteria for being blessed of God. Sometimes God will bless us in spite of ourselves because He loves us and because our hearts of repentance are sincere but in MOST cases God will not bless things that are done out of order. So we must learn how to let God get these issues worked out in our lives and be patient enough to endure the amount of time it will take to complete it.

We talked about microwave fulfillment earlier. The biggest seed of deception that the devil plants in each of our minds is the seed of impatience. He knows that if he can get us to operate in the spirit of impatience that we will make swift decisions without first consulting God. When we do this sometimes depending on the circumstance, we can get ourselves tangled up in a web that may take years and sometimes decades to unravel. When we follow the will of God to perfection we save ourselves the heartache and disappointment that comes with disobedience. We can avoid so many years of hurt, pain and embarrassment when we are obedient and when we do things God's way.

Getting Things Right

When we decide to get our lives right with God, we please Him. God wants to bless us. He is in the business of blessing His people. God wants to see us repent and get our lives back in good standing with Him. God wants to see each and every one of us remove our blinders and get back on the road to our divine destiny but He wants us to follow His established order.

When we decide to let God fix our lives and work things out in us, our lives flow much more peacefully. When Jonah made the decision to do as God had instructed him to do and preach to the people of Nineveh he was delivered from the mouth of the LARGE fish that swallowed him at the Lord's command. When He made the decision to obey God and do things God's way then he was delivered from his circumstance. So many of us are staying bound and oppressed by situations that God wants to deliver us out of. He just wants us to repent and get on the right path in good standing with Him. God wants to see you and I operating in the blessing of Almighty GOD. Nothing gives God more joy than to see His people doing what He created us to do. It grieves God when we don't obey Him and totally disregard His instruction.

In closing this chapter, we must realize that our own personal ambition can indeed cripple us. Although being ambitious is a good thing, we must learn how to control it and bring it under subjection and in line with God's plan for us. When we make that decision God will open up the floodgates of prosperity and bless us beyond our wildest imagination when the season is right.

Chapter 7

The Plot "Satan's Playbook"

I want to talk about something that the Holy Spirit revealed to me one morning during my intimate prayer time. He showed me that satan has a **PLAYBOOK** for every Christ Follower. He has specific strategies of deception and manipulation that he uses on each and every one of us to cause us to lose our spiritual authority.

That morning that I woke up I was discouraged because like so many times before, my lights had been cut off because of my financial struggles. I remember asking God "why does this keep happening to me? Why am I not getting ahead?' It seemed to me as if the same struggles were coming into my life year after year and I seemed to have NO victory over them. I could not understand how a man like me who read his bible, fasted and prayed constantly and had a personal relationship with Jesus could be living a constant life of frustration and defeat. It was not until the Holy Spirit revealed "Satan's PLOT" that morning that I began to understand what was going on in my life. Once God showed me what was happening, a HUGE RED LIGHT came on in my head. I thought to myself; "Wait a minute! You mean to tell me that satan has used the same playbook on me all of these years and I have not figured it out." As strange and condemning as it may seem, it is in fact true. The devil is truly not as clever as most of us may think. He simply plays on our weaknesses and takes advantage of them. He uses the same strategies over and over again. Unless you are aware of what is happening, you will never know what is going on in the spiritual realm. If you are a person who has problems with anger, He will always allow things to happen to you that will provoke you to become enraged and infuriated. Someone will always say something to you that will "push your buttons." If you are someone who is constantly **blinded** by fear, he will always allow things to happen to you that will cause you to be intimidated and afraid.

What do I do to get free?

I'm glad you asked that question. Here is the simple answer: You must simply **ASK** the Holy Spirit for revelation. Ask Him to reveal to you the things that are causing you to remain spiritually stagnant. I have found in my short life that the most difficult problems have simple solutions. When you ask God, He WILL give you revelation. When He shows you what the problems are, do not ignore them. Do not deny that you have problems in those areas because you will never obtain the freedom necessary to move forward. Embrace the fact that you have a problem and be thankful to God for showing it to you.

Make A List

That morning when God began to impart wisdom into me and give me understanding and clarity I began to write down everything that He revealed to me. As I put it on paper in PHYSICAL FORM I could see clearly what was happening and why I was living in spiritual bondage all of my life. When you are blinded by deception, you are committing purpose and destiny suicide. There is no way you can fulfill ALL that God has predestined you to fulfill if you are living a life of deception.

When I started writing down these things I began to see satan's playbook become exposed. I could see the cycle that was happening over and over in my life. Like clockwork the devil would always reveal him-self and begin using this playbook on my life. He would use the same strategies over and over again. He would use the same types of people, the same temptations and distractions to keep my focus off of the things that God was telling me to do. I was amazed at how I could miss all of this for so long. How could I not see what was happening to me?

When I began writing down my struggles, I began having peace and victory in my life as a result. The list gave me specific things to pray about. It showed me the areas in my life that I needed deliverance and victory in. When you write down your fears and concerns it causes you to face them HEAD ON.

I want to challenge each and every one of you to make that list. Get things out in the open and deal with those issues so that you can be all that GOD has purposed you to be. You are too smart, too anointed, and too blessed to remain deceived and manipulated by satan's playbook.

Whenever you are feeling yourself being bound by things that you seemed to have "victory over" again, go back and reference your list and pray over it diligently and watch what God will do in your life. You are a **LIST** away from a MAJOR breakthrough in your life.

Resist The Playbook!!!!

When you are being confronted and attacked by the things that you wrote on your list (and you can rest assured that you will) you must begin to resist those attacks. When they come to you this time you are no longer ignorant of them. You have to open up your mouth and declare and decree that you will NEVER BE BOUND BY THIS AGAIN!!!! When you say it, you've got to MEAN IT. Your freedom depends on it. You have to be sick and tired of allowing your life to be manipulated and controlled by the same strategies and games. You have to make it be known that you will no longer tolerate these **blinders** and deception of the adversary. You are a GREAT man or woman of faith and you have the POWER to resist these attacks.

You can end this cycle beginning TODAY. The choice is up to you whether you will begin living a life of freedom or whether you will continue on living a life of deception. Make the LIST and speak victory over your life. You have the power and you will overcome.

CHAPTER 8

SELF-FORGIVENESS

In removing the blinders that block us from receiving what God has for us and His divine purpose for our lives, we must grasp the concept of **self-forgiveness**. In this chapter we will discuss various ways that the enemy will use the guilt of past failures to keep us from receiving what God has for our lives. We will also discuss how we can overcome these feelings of guilt and unworthiness with the word of God.

Guilt

The first way the enemy can keep us from receiving what God has for us is guilt. Often times the reason why we are in the predicament that we are in is because of the poor life choices that we have made. The reality is that if we had not made certain decisions, we would not be facing the difficulties that we face. We feel guilty because of our "own" bad choices. Often times this feeling of guilt will lower our self-esteem and lower our level of confidence.

Often times we will find ourselves being overtaken by a spirit of unworthiness. We feel as though God will not bless us because the mistake or mistakes that we made are too great. In God's eyes there is no such thing as an unforgivable mistake with the only exception being blasphemy. If you have not blasphemed against the Holy Spirit then you are FORGIVEN. It is satan's responsibility to keep us dwelling in that area of guilt for past failures and mistakes. By keeping us here, he can keep our self-esteem low. We discussed where God's word says in

Hebrews chapter 10 that we should not throw away our confidence.

Our confidence is our strength. Our main weapons are our confidence and faith as believers. We have to constantly remind ourselves that we are fearfully and wonderfully made (Psalm 139:14). God made no mistake when he created you. He created you with a specific purpose in mind. He does not want you to stay bound by guilt. When you make a mistake, all He wants you to do is repent and He will do the rest. God is a restorer. God will restore and redeem those whom He loves.

I remember when I was a young man growing up in the church, the older saints used to always tell us to "turn it over to Jesus". At the time I used to laugh at what they were saying because I heard that so much. I had heard that message so many times that I had become immune to it. But when I really began to find myself as an adult in situations that I needed God to deliver me from and search God's word, I realized that God wanted me to give Him my burdens to carry. I began to have an understanding of what God's love, grace, and mercy was all about.

Shame

Another way that the enemy can keep us from being used of God at full capacity is by keeping us bound by **shame**. The shame is usually associated with something that we have done wrong in the past.

Some things in our lives make us ashamed of what we have done. Sometimes we feel so ashamed of what we have done that we do not even want to show our faces. We feel embarrassed and unloved because of what we have done. Some secrets about our past frighten us and keep us from seeking the face of God because of the guilt and shame of it all. Sometimes we fail to realize that God can take the very thing that we are "ashamed of" and use it as a testimony for someone who is going through a similar situation.

Mind over Circumstance and Opinion

In my life I have adopted the principle of *"mind over circumstance and opinion."* Often times the enemy can keep us bound in self-pity and unforgiveness by using two weapons against us: Circumstance and Opinion.

Circumstance

Sometimes our circumstances can cause us to be ashamed and embarrassed. This could be our surroundings, neighborhood we live in, job we work etc. For instance, we feel as though we should be further along in life or should have achieved a better degree in school so that we could have a better job than the one that we currently have. We feel ashamed of the fact that we work waiting tables at a restaurant when we thought that we would be the CEO of a fortune 500 company. Our circumstance has now defined us and we are ashamed of our current state. Instead of looking at the good and seeking the God who can change any circumstance, we focus on the here and now and allow it to discourage us. Instead of us being grateful to God for giving us a job period, we focus on the fact that we don't have the job that WE want. As a result we make bad decisions based on how we feel people will perceive us.

Opinion

For so many years of my life I allowed people's opinion of me to define who I was as a man. I would try to do things and say things that would make people accept me better. I let it affect every aspect of my life. I was even ashamed of how I talked. I have a very deep and raspy voice and my peers at school and at work would always try to make me feel self-conscious about it. I would try to purposefully change my speech patterns and voice tonality because I did not want to be ridiculed at school.

Instead of embracing the very characteristics that God gave me that made me unique and special, I was ashamed and embarrassed of them because I was bound by others' opinion of me. I can remember when I was completely freed from that low self esteem and concern about people's opinion of me. It was the most liberating experience of my life. I realized my uniqueness was special to God and that voice was given to me by God for a specific purpose and calling.

When God called me to ministry I realized the importance of having that voice. I travel this country preaching and teaching God's word because of my voice. I now make a living and support my family because of that voice that GOD had given me. We must learn to embrace our uniqueness and not allow fear of people's opinion to set the tone for how we live our lives.

Understanding God's Forgiveness

Let's take a closer look into the mercy and forgiveness of God. As stated earlier we discussed how when we are full of shame and guilt we feel as though we are not worthy to be forgiven by God. God's word tells us that His mercy is **EVERLASTING**. This means that there is no end to God's mercy and grace. God knew before He created us that we would have failures in our lives. He knew that we would fall short of His expectations of us. God, even in His sovereignty, realizes that we are in human flesh and have the capacity to fall short. Although He created us to serve Him, he also realizes that we can sometimes fall into sin.

All God wants is repentance, that's it. Once we have repented our sins are forgiven, no questions asked. God 's word tells us that He will cast our sins in the sea of forgetfulness never to be remembered again. The 51st Psalm is the ultimate prayer of repentance that we must follow as believers. Although King David committed a horrible sin, his heart was sincere in his petition to God. He had the mindset that he had betrayed God and that he had a desire not to fall again. Although he still had to pay a hefty price for the mistake that he made, God still forgave him and continued to show him favor.

We as believers must understand that even though God forgives us sometimes there are costs that are associated with our decisions to sin. This is why it is very important to stay on the RIGHT path. When we steer away from our paths that God has laid out for us we can cause ourselves a great deal of difficulty and stress. It is better to stay in God's perfect will and get the FULL benefits of what he has for your life but if you do however fall short of God's expectations it's not the end of your life. God is still working things out in your life. He wants to complete what he started and you must allow him to (*Philippians 1:6*).

God does not hold grudges. He is merciful and kind. The sacrifice of His son Jesus freed us from the penalty of sin. Jesus came and died so that our sins would be forgiven and that we would have life eternally. Satan desires to keep us at a place where we feel victimized by our past mistakes and failures. He wants us to lose our since of value in the kingdom of God. It is extremely important for you to realize that you are valuable to God. You are a jewel in God's eyes. Your life means so much more to God than you can even imagine. His love for us exceeds our wildest thoughts and imagination. If we only knew just how valuable and special we were to God, we would not treat ourselves the way that we do.

Satan wants to destroy you before you reach your full potential. He will use any and every tool to abort what God is trying to birth out of you and through you. This is why he is so hard at work. He will use our peers, "friends", family, and co-workers to intimidate you and make you lose your authority and position as a Christ follower.

Our confidence in God is a key component in our walk with Christ. Our confidence is not in our own abilities but rather in Christ's ability to keep us. (*Jude 1:24*) We must understand God's keeping power. If we desire to be kept from sin, God will keep us. Satan wants you to buy into the concept that everyone is sinning and that everyone is doing wrong. He wants you to believe that everyone is lying, cheating, stealing and committing adultery.

There is so much garbage on television that I hardly watch it anymore. It is full of immorality and iniquity. When we flood our mind with things that do not uplift our spirit and bring us in closer fellowship with Christ then we are open prey to the enemy's attack and his devices. It is almost as though we are on the football field of life playing without pads. Ephesians 6 tells us to be on guard and to arm ourselves with the things of God. We must always be prepared for pitfalls and snares.

We cannot afford to allow ourselves to become entangled in self-righteousness. It is when we become self-righteous that we are the most vulnerable. This is usually when we pray the least, when we God's word the least, and when we fast and meditate the least. Humility is a **MUST** when it comes to walking with Christ. God's word tells us that the meek shall inherit the earth. God loves humility. When we walk in humility we allow God to exalt us to the level that He desires for us to be. Sometimes our own ego can prevent us from achieving and receiving all God has for us. When we get out of the way and allow God to work through us we become much more effective in our gifts and callings.

God's word tells us to lay aside every weight and sin that easily entangles us. (*Hebrews 12:1*) Often times these weights can be pride and arrogance. These things will cause us to miss our blessings. When we really analyze pride and arrogance, it is actually a form of idolatry because when we are giving in to those spirits, we are in a sense "worshiping ourselves". Anything that takes priority over God in our lives is a god. Although we may not be verbally confessing that we are worshipping ourselves, our fruits clearly show that we are by the way that we behave. When we spend more time grooming ourselves and admiring ourselves than we spend in God's presence we are idolizing ourselves in my opinion. I am not making the argument that we are not supposed to keep our bodies clean and pure nor am I saying that we should not admire our accomplishments but rather pointing out the fact that those things should not take priority over our time in God's presence. God's time is valuable and precious and should in no way be tampered or interfered with.

The more time we spend worshipping God, the more that He reveals to us. The more we fast and pray, the stronger we become and the less spirits we become exposed to. God will give us wisdom to see danger before it arrives. When we spend time wallowing in arrogance we eliminate that ability because we have not tapped into the source that provides that kind of insight.

I want to close this chapter by saying that you owe it to yourself to forgive yourself. Nothing that you have done is so bad that it does not warrant God's forgiveness. God loves you and I and He wants what is best for us. He loves you and cherishes everything about you. Allow God to love you and forgive you. You are worth that much and more to Him.

CHAPTER 9

GET MOTIVATED AND GET TO WORK

In this chapter we will deal with how lack of motivation and despondency can cause us to be **blinded** from operating in what God has purposed for our lives. We will discuss how to overcome adversity and failures and get back on track. We will explore ways that the enemy will try to keep us from recovering and refocusing. We will also address ways in which we can get back on track and get refocused on our goal. We will look at different ways the enemy can influence us and take our confidence and motivation.

I will start by using my own personal testimony. When I first started to get an idea of what God wanted me to do with my life I was overwhelmed with passion and desire. I was highly driven and motivated. I went out and started printing up business cards, scheduling events and networking with people who were like-minded. I was doing everything to prepare myself for what I was going to do. I thought that God would bless my ministry and prosper me right away and then reality began to set in.

I quickly started to realize just how LONG the road to success was. I began to realize that the very same people who were once cheering me on to achieve that success were now stabbing me in the back and ridiculing me. The pain of failure and misfortune weighed heavily on me and I began to slip in and out of depression because of it. I lost ALL motivation and just began to sit around my house doing absolutely nothing. I began wasting valuable time. I was so disappointed because of the rejections that I was receiving. It seemed like every attempt that I made at my goals was being rejected. The more I tried the more I was rejected.

I quickly became "burnt out". I was also dealing with some misfortunes in my personal life. I started to second-guess myself, not only as a man of God but also as a MAN period. As a result of my ministry not being as prosperous as I had expected it to be, I started to struggle financially. I had given up working "regular" jobs so that I could pursue the ministry full-time. Needless to say things didn't turn out as I planned and my finances, including my credit suffered greatly. I was a single father and could not even support my children. I felt like less of a man.

All of my hopes and dreams seemed to be shattered. From time to time I had to swallow my pride and go back and work regular part-time jobs just to make ends meet. Although I was a staffed worker at my church, I still didn't make enough to support my family, not to mention I had virtually no financial support from the mother of my children. This made me frustrated, angry and depressed for so many years. It even affected my weight. I physically suffered as my weight ballooned to well over 300 lbs. I had never been that heavy in my life before.

I had to face the harsh reality that I was dealing with depression. I needed to be motivated and I had absolutely no motivation. One day I stumbled across a life-changing message that I found on YouTube. That sermon dealt with rising above despondency and depression. It dealt with overcoming slothfulness and unconcern. I had to face the fact that I was being controlled and oppressed by those spirits for so long that I thought they were a permanent part of my behavior. I no longer knew who I was and who's I was. I had also become a hoarder. I had let everything around me fall apart. My apartment had become a garbage pit. The condition of my house was a reflection of what was going on inside of my heart. Many times what we see on the exterior of a person is a mirror image of what they are dealing with internally.

I did not even realize that I was being oppressed by familiar spirits. These spirits had controlled me for so long. The reason I was being oppressed is because I ALLOWED MYSELF TO BE! I lost my position of authority and lost my identity in Christ and thus I became a slave to these spirits. Once I heard that word, my heart was convicted and God began the liberation process within me.

When I heard that message and my spirit was convicted I found what I thought was myself getting angry but it was my flesh and those contrary spirits fighting against the will of God. The more I listened to the man speak to my situation the more convicted I became. He was "hitting me where it hurt." My pride, my spirit, and my will were being broken. Although I did not like what was being said, I knew I had to endure it because I knew that what was being said was for my good.

So I continued to listen. The more I yielded, the more I felt myself begin to become free from those spirits. Tears rolled down my face and I began to thank God for allowing me to see where I was in error. If we seek God He will reveal what is blocking our blessings and favor.

What I found is that when our faults are exposed God can deal with the core of the problem. Our pride must be completely stripped in order for God to change us. If we are still holding on to our pride then we limit God's effectiveness in our lives. It's not that God does not have the ability to change us we just do not allow Him to. Remember God will not impose His will on anyone. He gives us all free will and free choice.

Many times we do not receive all that God has for us because we do not get to work and allow

Him to use us. It's great for each of us to have a plan and to dream but the bible also tells us that our faith will not work for us without our effort. (*James 2:17*) You have to put work behind your faith "hustle behind your muscle." When I received that life-changing message, I realized that I was allowing the spirit of laziness to overtake me. I did not want to admit that I was lazy. That really hurt my pride. When I received my correction and rebuke I felt renewed and refreshed. I could no longer blame life circumstances or the mistreatment of others. I had to address the man who was staring at me in the mirror.

No one wants to admit that they are lazy, especially men. Most men want to be perceived as hard-workers and providers but the bible tells us that we know a tree by its fruit. So in other words if it looks like a duck and quacks like a duck it's a duck. If you are acting like a lazy person, chances are YOU ARE.

If you are not working, you WILL NOT receive anything. God's word also tells us that a lazy man does not deserve to eat. You cannot sit around the house watching reality television and surfing the web all day and expect God to use your gift. If you are not making yourself available to be used, God will not use you. He will simply pass you and move on to someone who is willing to put in the WORK. When we are slothful we disappoint God. He is not pleased with this SINFUL lifestyle. When I was a child, my mother would never allow my sister and me to stay in the bed past 8 a.m. on Saturdays and even during our "summer vacations." We had to be up cleaning our rooms, doing yard work or something. You had to be doing something. If you weren't doing some type of chore you had better be outside getting some exercise.

The problem with today's generation is we want to sleep, sleep, and sleep. Some of us will sleep our way right away from God's blessings for our lives. If you can't find a job right away, keep looking. Don't give up. Most of the time the best things in life require a great deal of effort and perseverance. God is not pleased with us when we operate in the spirit of laziness. God cannot and will not use someone who is lazy. It does not work that way.

Often times we will say that we are not moving because we do not know which way we should go. God wants us to **GET UP** and seek out what He wants. For so many years of my life, I sat on the couch waiting on God to drop an answer out of heaven when He wanted me to get up and **FIND** the answer. The scriptures tell us to SEEK and we shall FIND. If you don't seek you will NEVER find. There must be an **ACTION** in order for God to cause a **REACTION** to take place.

Depression and Despondency

Let's take a moment to analyze the spirit of depression. We know that it does in fact come from satan. God's word tells us that every GOOD and PERFECT gift comes from God and God only. So if what we are experiencing is neither good nor perfect, it cannot be from God. Depression is an evil spirit. It is a state in which satan tries to keep us in. When he keeps us operating in a state of depression, he knows that we have no authority or confidence because there is a great reward in our confidence.

Remember when we analyzed God's word in Hebrews 10 where it talks about not casting away our confidence. When we yield to the spirit of depression we forfeit our confidence therefore there is no reward. The enemy's job is to keep us depressed and despondent. God's word tells us that God in us is greater than He that is in the world. God's word also tells us that we are MORE than conquerors. When we realize our authority and who we belong to it is extremely difficult to fall into the deception (blinder) of depression. The spirit of depression can, however creep up on anyone if they are not resisting it.

Depression yields laziness. Have you ever noticed that most people who are lazy are usually depressed and despondent all of the time. They usually always need someone to encourage them or speak a word into their life. People who are lazy usually want someone to take care of them and pick up their slack. They usually want people to feel sorry for them.

Where there is laziness there is usually lack of faith. When I was being controlled by that spirit, I was always negative all of the time. It was hard to be around me. Even if things were going well in my life, I was always wondering if some misfortune was lurking around the corner ready to pounce on me at any moment. When the trials of life did finally manifest, I was always making evil declarations over my life. I was confessing that I deserved what was happening.

You must always watch what you confess. Even when you do deserve what you get you must realize that God is a forgiving and merciful God who gives second chances. When you confess failure and poverty over your life, you give satan the power to control you. You give him the keys to the car. You should NEVER relinquish your authority no matter how difficult life gets. You must always confess positivity over your life. You must say things such as; " I may not be where I want to be but I will get through this because God's word declares I will." When you make these types of declarations you take the authority away from satan and put it right back into your hands.

Don't stay where you are and wallow in laziness and depression, rise up and take your rightful inheritance as a joint heir with Christ Jesus. Don't sit around and feel sorry for yourself, **GET UP AND DO SOMETHING!!!!** Ask God what His will and desire is for your life. When He gives you an answer don't let fear of failure control you.

Remember that the Joy of the Lord is your strength.

Get Back On Track

If you have fallen short and lost your way it is never too late to get back on track and allow God to pick up where He left off in your life. If you have dropped your vision, pick it back up. Get back in the race. Repent and get back to work. Repeat this prayer aloud with me: *"Lord I know that I have come short of your expectations for my life. I ask you to forgive me and cleanse me with the blood of your beloved son Jesus. Give me a new start and clear vision. I declare this day that I am NO LONGER a lazy man or woman. I know who I am and who's I am. I claim back my authority and my position. Use me to the fullest. Give me a clearer*

understanding for what you want out of my life
than you ever have before. In Jesus' name Amen."

Once you have confessed this prayer do NOT give back your authority. Claim it and keep it. Guard it with your life. God will use you again as if you never lost time. I believe that when we get things right with God, He always makes ALL things new. It is as though we never came up short. When God gives you another chance make Him proud. Run the race with confidence and spiritual authority. Be bold. When one door closes, expect the next one to be wide open. Pray for favor and divine appointments. Ask God to make **provisions** concerning your **vision**. Be specific about what you want God to do for you. Allow Him to use you in the way that He desires to use you. Don't be afraid of success. Remember you will never know unless you try.

CHAPTER 10

KNOWING HOW TO BE USED EFFECTIVELY

In this chapter we will discuss the importance of knowing how to allow God to use us when we are in the season for Him to fully use us. We will discuss the ways in which we can effectively hear from God about what to do and how to pray and ask God for provisions and divine appointments that will set us in a place to effectively flow in our gifts and callings.

What I have discovered is that many times when our season has arrived and we are fully aware of what God wants to do through our lives we do not fully understand how to go about doing what God has called us to do. We are simply trying to figure things out with no plan or strategy. We just simply find ourselves "winging it" with no game plan.

When you have no organized plan or strategy, you can get confused and distracted. Every level of success in life requires order and discipline. You should have a vision board or an outline for your success. Although I am very aware that God can change our plans and put His stamp on them, we should still have guidelines and rules that help keep us disciplined and on task. If you desire to succeed, you should have an accountability system in place. The accountability system may consist of setting uncompromised goals and deadlines for yourself or simply having groups of friends who keep you accountable.

We talked about Habakkuk 2:2 earlier. We briefly addressed writing down our vision and making it plain. You should have something in physical form that you can go back and reference when you fall into distraction from time to time. It is a must that you have a plan when you are building your model for success. Never forget the fact that even though God is at work and wants to see you prosper, He still wants you to have a well-organized strategy.

Don't lose your integrity

I can't help but notice how so many people in "the ministry" are only concerned with getting elevated to higher positions. In the church organization that I grew up in I would see pastors arguing and debating over getting elevated and promoted to new **TITLES**. What amazed me is how these so called pastors would show blatant disrespect towards one another and compete heavily for positions and when they would finally get their "promotion" they were not even willing to do the work that the "title" required. All they cared about was getting promoted to a higher position and they would almost stop at nothing to get those positions. Sometimes even at the expense of their families. To make matters worse, when they would get these "promotions" they would have the unmitigated gumption to thank God for blessing them with those promotions after they had hooked, crooked, and scammed their way into them. Once the election for promotion against their counterparts in the gospel had concluded, they would try to smooth things over and act as if they had not broken the code of ethics with NO repentance or apology to the people they hurt in the process. It was mind-blowing to me.

So much emphasis is being placed on titles and promotion that we have forgotten the God who makes provisions for us to get those titles and be promoted. When God makes provisions for us we do not have to **FORCE** our way to the top. God's word tells us that promotion comes from above. Quite honestly our priorities are altogether wrong if we conduct ourselves in this way. We should be more concerned with being salt and light and making a difference in a dark world than getting the recognition and accolades of people.

Make Yourself Available

When you are experiencing what I like to call "downtime," it is important not to lose patience and get discouraged. Because when you start worrying, you become non-productive. You start worrying about what everyone else is doing and not focusing on what God requires and **demands** of you.

It is extremely important for us during this time not to allow the blinders of anxiety and passion overtake us. When we become overzealous often times we make irrational decisions based on our emotions and impulses. I have seen so many people be in a season in which God was about to use them in a mighty way but they could not exercise patience nor self-control and made hasty decisions that set them back for many years. If they would have just allowed God to promote them and do things the right way they would have been much more effective and fruitful.

Let Go Of The Wheel And Put Your Ego Aside

This is an area that we all struggle with. We all feel as though we have the answers and although we may not verbally confess it, often times we think we know more than God does about us. Instead of allowing Him to move us in a perfect way, we try to take control of the situation by getting in the way of God. We start trying to promote ourselves and we try to allow our egos and self-confidence to become greater than God. The Apostle Paul wrote; *"I can do all things through **CHRIST** who strengthens me* (Philippians 4:13). We must realize as Christ followers that we can only accomplish things through Christ and Christ alone. He does not need any help from us. Remember when we discussed having confidence in an earlier chapter, the confidence is not in our own abilities and talents, but rather in the GOD that gives us those abilities and talents. So when we confess that we can do ALL things through Christ, then the emphasis should be on CHRIST and not ourselves.

Our egos and self-pride are major **blinders** that satan uses to keep our focus away from God. When we start looking at our own abilities and hard work as the catalyst for our success then we make ourselves vulnerable to snares and pitfalls. When we maintain the spirit of humility then we allow God to take complete control of our lives. We give Him all of the authority that He deserves. God's word tells us that Jesus is the author and finisher of our faith. That means without Christ there is no success. The word authority is a derivative of the word author. So if Christ is the author then he should have complete authority over our lives. We must allow God to author our lives. We are the book and He is the author. He wants to write the greatest novel ever written and He wants you to be the main character. He wants to write YOUR success story. He wants to author a story of tests and trials that lead to your triumphant ending.

He just wants you to be available for Him to do so. I make a point when I am praying before each sermon that I preach to always make the declaration that *God you are the author, take my tongue and use it as the pen of a ready writer.* In other words I am asking God to take control of the words that I speak and to inspire everything that I say to His people. I also ask God to give me a word that will impact, inspire, and provoke change. When we pray a sincere prayer to God and allow Him FULL control over our gifts and talents there is no limit to where He can and will take us. He just wants our availability.

Take On The Attitude of A Good Listener

Quite candidly this is still something that I struggle with sometimes. If we are all honest with ourselves this is something that MOST Christ followers struggle with. Many times God is trying to give us wisdom and instruction and we do not take heed. We don't listen to what He is trying to tell us and we reject his wisdom and instruction. It is extremely important for us to take on the attitude of a listener and not always be someone who engages in excessive talking. God's word tells us to be *quick to listen, slow to speak and slow to become angry James 1:19.* So many times we block our blessings because we do not wait for instruction. God told king David when he inquired about the second encounter with the Philistine Army to wait for a sound of marching in the mulberry trees before you attack them. If David had not listened to God's instruction they would have lost that war. Two things about that passage really struck me. First of all David INQUIRED and then God RESPONDED! Often times we do not ask God for wisdom and instruction. We don't seek His face for instruction concerning just **HOW** He wants us to pursue our purpose. The second point to note is that God Responded. When He responded David **LISTENED**. When we pray we must meditate and wait for an answer from God. We must not spend our entire time dumping our problems and concerns on God and not allow Him to respond.

It is very true that we must take our burdens and concerns to the Lord, but it's also true that we must allow Him to speak to us so that we can get a clear understanding of what He desires. Remember we discussed James 1:5 in an earlier chapter. If you lack wisdom ask God and He will make things clear for your understanding. The critical part of this analysis is asking. When we ask we will receive and when it is time to receive, we must receive. Allow me to briefly clarify that statement. Sometimes we ask God for wisdom about a decision that we face and we follow all of the steps that I just mentioned. We pray and seek Him for wisdom, we listen and He responds. The conundrum that we face is that when He does respond, we do not receive what He is telling us. In other words his response may not be favorable to us so we turn a deaf ear to it or act as though He never responded when we clearly know that He did and we know EXACTLY what His answer was.

There are so many people who are still "seeking God" for answers that He gave them clarity on a long time ago. If you know that God told you not to marry that man, STOP asking Him for an answer. He already said NO. If we are really honest with ourselves, the real issue that we have is that we did not get the answer that we desire so we continue to "pray about it" and hope that God will change His mind. There are some things that God protects us from and He will NEVER compromise on. God sees things that we don't see. He knows that we cannot handle certain things. Even though we may feel as though we can handle them, we should let go and realize that God knows more than we do and that He does in fact know what is best for us. God created us and He knows our habits, likes, dislikes and attitudes. He knows what we can bare. He loves us and as a result He will shield us from what we perceive as "success." There have been countless times in my life that I wished that I had listened to God When He warned me about some things. After I did not listen and fell flat on my face, I began to cry out for forgiveness and mercy. The problem was that I did not listen the first time. I could have saved myself from a lot of wrath and judgment but I chose not to As a result, I paid a tremendous price.

Let us not forget to trust God. He has all of the answers. When He speaks, we must listen and then respond accordingly. God gets the glory when we respond to Him with obedience and humility. He can work with us when we take on this attitude.

Ask God For Provisions and Divine Appointments

When we are trying to flow in our gifts and callings and be used greatly of God, we must develop the habit of asking for favor and provisions. When God gives favor and provisions, He gives us a VIP pass into an overflow of blessings and prosperity in abundance. I have learned not to ask for wealth but to rather pray for favor and provisions. When we have favor, God opens door after door after door. It sometimes feels as though no one can harm you nor even touch you. When you have favor the devil can do nothing to stop what God has ordained. He may try but he will be unsuccessful.

The enemy also gets fearful and intimidated when we have favor. Some of us have an abundance of favor and don't even realize what we have. I am a firm believer that the reason why the devil has tried to throw so many firey darts in my direction is the fact that he knows that I have favor and he is trying to abort what God is trying to birth in me. Saul threw a javelin at David in hopes that he would kill him before God would birth destiny and purpose in him. The spear was thrown out of spite and jealousy. The devil is jealous of your purpose and destiny. He wants to confuse, intimidate and scare you out of what God has purposed for you.

Many times we do not have favor and divine appointments because we simply do not ask for them. When we pray we must ask for specific needs Philippians 4:6 tells us to make our request be known. In other words we must be specific in our requests. When we are specific with our prayer requests it gives us a *"point of emphasis"*. When you are praying for something to happen, you have to "give it a name." When you confess it you allow yourself to speak life into it. Just as you pray for things and believe God for things you should confess them and speak them into being. Proverbs 18:21 tells us that death and life are in the power of the tongue. Make your request know and then begin to speak it over your life. You have to tell yourself "I am blessed and highly favored of God, I am an anointed man or woman of God, Wealth and riches are in my house, This is my season to be used greatly by God."

I like to confess these things by turning a negative into a positive. The more I do not see them manifested in my life, the more I decree and declare that they are. You have to be bold in your declarations. God responds only to positivity. Have you ever noticed that when a person is negative, they affect everyone around them. I don't like being around negative people. When I see them coming, I run the other way. If we are children of the most-high king we have no reason to be negative when God will provide us with whatever we need. In a previous chapter we talked about inheritance with Christ. When we realize that God has established this world and created us to serve Him and live for Him then it is easier to realize our value. Every morning when you wake out of bed tell yourself "I am valuable to God." God values us and loves us far beyond what we can even imagine. God thinks so greatly of us that He sacrificed His only begotten (John 3:16).

In closing I want to paint a picture in your mind of a merciful and loving God that wants to see you succeed. God does not want you to miss your season. He is, in fact, pulling for you. God wants to get the glory out of your life. He wants to use you greatly in every aspect of your life. Our gifts and talents are vehicles that God uses for His glory and to bring lost souls into the kingdom. God has not forgotten you. He wants to use you. He just wants you to make yourself available and do things in the RIGHT season and with honesty and integrity.

CHAPTER 11

UNBLINDFOLDED

I want to begin this chapter by addressing a miracle that Jesus performed in the 8th chapter of the book of St. Mark in which Jesus healed a blind man in Bethsaida. Here we learn of a man that the people bring to Jesus who is blind. The people begged Jesus to touch the man and heal him but Jesus decided to heal the man in an unconventional way. The bible tells us that Jesus took the man by the hand and carried him out of the village. Jesus spat in the man's eyes and laid His hands on him and asked if he had seen anything and the man replied "yes I can see them but not clearly. They look like trees walking around". So Jesus placed his hands on the man's eyes again and suddenly the man opened his eyes again and he could now see clearly.

Many of us are like the blind man at Bethsaida. We have walked around blinded for so many years. We are not able to see clearly and suddenly we have an encounter with Jesus. He begins to make everything clear in our lives. This is what happens when we allow God to remove the blindfolds from our eyes. When we allow Him to heal us from the bondage of deception, we get a clear view of life. It is almost as fascinating as the feeling that you had when you were first born again and accepted Christ as your personal Lord and Savior.

I remember when I had the blinders removed from my eyes. I felt as though I was a man that had been a slave of deception for so many years of my life but when God gave me complete insight and revelation, I felt renewed and refreshed. Let us take a moment to analyze the story of Jesus and the blind man at Bethsaida. I want to point out a couple of points to this story that relate to what we as Christians in pursuit of our purpose encounter when we reach the period of insight and liberation from satan's deception.

When we look at this account in scripture we see that a couple of things had to happen in order for Jesus to completely liberate and heal this man who was blind. First of all Jesus had to remove him from his surroundings. Many people who preach and teach from this passage leave out this important point. There was a reason why Jesus had to remove him from his surroundings. Often times God has to remove us from family members, bad relationships, unwise council, and toxic friendships to remove our blinders of deception. In many cases these people who "mean us well" are more harmful than helpful. When we are exposed to their negativity and lack of faith and wisdom it can adversely affect our own confidence in God's ability. We must distance ourselves from these types of people and relationships. They can do nothing but cause us harm. Sometimes these people are a constant reminder of what we used to be. God wants to transform us into what He wants us to be. God's word tells us that if we are in Christ we are a **NEW creation** and the old things are gone.

Once God got the man away from his old neighborhood and his peers then He was able to perform a miracle in his life. So many of us are not allowing God to change us and enlighten us. He wants to remove those blinders from our eyes and give us insight but we don't allow Him to. We are resisting the will of God. We still want to hang on to those bad habits and bad company that have kept us bound for so many years. God wants to do a new thing in your life. When God is changing your surroundings don't allow fear to control you. Sometimes fear of the unknown can be our biggest enemy. We are not sure where God is taking us so we try to hang on to our old season when God is trying to move us into a new one. Tell yourself that fear must die so that God can take you where He desires for you to go.

Also after Jesus takes the man out of his comfortable surroundings He does something unusual. He literally spits in the man's eyes. I am a firm believer that if the man would have remained in that village, so many people would have been questioning His healing methods and caused the man to have doubt in what God was doing. Once the distractions were gone Jesus began to perform this miracle. The spitting in the eyes is symbolic in my opinion. It represents how God does certain things in our lives that we may not particularly agree with. He sometimes uses unconventional methods to provoke change and deliverance. The man did not question Christ's healing methods, he just knew that he needed something from God and he was not going to leave until he received it. What I have found is that if we really want God to do something for us and through us, we will endure whatever comes our way in order to receive from God.

When you read down in the passage, you will also notice that Jesus laid hands on the man's eyes and when He removed them He asked the man what he saw. The man responded by saying Lord I now see but I still cannot see clearly. He explained to Jesus that it appears as though there are trees walking around. Now I am sure that the man was glad to be able to see period, but He wanted a COMPLETE healing to take place.

So many times God begins working things out in our lives and gives us clarity concerning His desires for us. Unfortunately we often times do not allow Him to **complete our transformation**. It is almost as though we are only partially un-blindfolded. We are walking around **partially delivered**. We would rather accept a **PARTIAL** blessing than a **COMPLETE** one. We continue to wonder through life aimlessly. We will continue to be deceived with only a partial revelation. I believe that Jesus was testing the man to find out if he would be honest and sincere about his condition. I am a firm believer that if this man would have accepted only a partial miracle that Jesus would have left him in the condition that he was in. I also believe that GOD loves a sincere and contrite heart. When this man was honest about his condition then Jesus was able to COMPLETE what he had started in the man's life. It is a must that we allow Christ to complete what He begins in our life. Allow him complete control so that he can completely remove the blindfolds from your eyes. No one wants to walk around living the rest of their lives deceived neither does God want us to be that way.

When we are un-blindfolded we are completely liberated. All distractions and deceptions have been removed. As a result, we can begin the process of doing what we have been ordained and commissioned to do. There is no greater feeling than knowing that you are operating in the complete and divine will of God. When this takes place just watch how smoothly you will be able to flow in the anointing. Watch how many lives will be changed because of the power of God working in you and through you. It will almost feel as though very little effort and exertion is required. This is how you will know that you are operating in the complete and divine will of God.

In closing I would like to confess this prayer over your life: *Dear Lord I thank you for your son Jesus and the sacrifice He paid on the cross for my sin. I thank you for giving me life, health, strength, wisdom and most of all unconditional love. I thank you for removing the blinders from my eyes and allowing me to see clearly and have a full understanding of your will and purpose for my life. Use me to the best of my abilities and beyond. Be glorified in everything that I achieve and accomplish. I pray these blessings in the name of your dear son Jesus' name Amen.*